A HANDBOOK

OF THE

FIGHTING RACES OF INDIA.

A HANDBOOK

OF THE

FIGHTING RACES OF INDIA.

BY

P. D. BONARJEE,

Assistant in the Military Department of the Govt. of India.

———

The Naval & Military Press Ltd

Published by

The Naval & Military Press Ltd

Unit 5 Riverside, Brambleside
Bellbrook Industrial Estate
Uckfield, East Sussex
TN22 1QQ England

Tel: +44 (0)1825 749494

www.naval-military-press.com
www.nmarchive.com

*In reprinting in facsimile from the original, any imperfections are inevitably reproduced
and the quality may fall short of modern type and cartographic standards.*

Dedicated

CONTENTS.

PREFACE.

In this little book I have attempted to give a brief sketch of the history, ethnology, customs, characteristics, etc., of the fighting races of India, so as to give the young British officer an idea of the material of which the native army is composed. There are several works extant dealing with the martial races of the country, such as those of Brian Hodgson, Dr. Wright, Genl. Cunningham, and others ; but these are as a rule not easily available, and are moreover technical expositions meant for historical and scientific purposes rather than practical treatises for the practical soldier.

The need of a book of this sort is acknowledged in military circles, and of late years, attempts to supply information regarding particular classes have not been wanting. Capt. Vansittart's book on Gurkhas, and Capt. R. W. Falcon's book on Sikhs, are excellent works on those races. Capt. A. H. Bingley, of the 7th Rajputs, is also preparing a series of class handbooks of the Indian Army, and official copies of the handbooks on 'Brahmans' and 'Rajputs' have been recently issued. But no attempt has been made, so far as I am aware, to deal with the fighting races of India as a whole ; and it is hoped this book will prove a suitable text-book to put into the hands of young officers. It was begun several years ago, but circumstances prevented its completion till lately.

I have omitted all those thousand and one details regarding the various races and castes dealt with, which, however useful they may be for the recruiting officer, are not necessary for an intelligent and comprehensive grasp of the subject. The present work can only be regarded as an introductory treatise on the subject. All it professes to supply is a clear and brief account of the fighting material of the country, for the use of young British officers.

A word of warning is necessary in regard to the location of the Pathan tribes, which has in many cases been given approximately only. It is not possible to describe accurately and fully the location of all the various tribes, as that would require in many cases references to geographical details which appear only on confidential maps.

I have drawn up a list of books for the use of officers desiring further information; and I must at the same time acknowledge my indebtedness to many of the authorities there quoted ; especially to Mr. Ibbetson of the Indian Civil Service, whose Punjab Census Report of 1881 forms an invaluable guide for the ethnologist.

MILITARY DEPT.,　}
Simla, the 1st Sept. 1899. }　　　　　　P. D. B.

AUTHORITIES

IBBETSON, Mr. D. J. C.—Punjab Census Report of 1881.

MACLAGAN, Mr. E. D.—Punjab Census Report of 1891.

BELLEW, Surgn.-Genl.—Races of Afghanistan.

       ,,   ,,   Yusufzai.

CUNNINGHAM, Genl.—Archæological Reports, Vol. II.

GRIFFIN, Sir L.—Punjab Chiefs.

MINCHIN, Capt. C.—Memorandum on the Baluch Tribes in the Dera Ghazi Khan District.

BRUCE R. I.—Notes on the Deraghazi Khan District, N.-W. Frontier and Border Tribes.

Report on the Kohat Pass Afridis.

Gazeteer of the Delhi District.

                 ,, Umballa District.

                 ,, Amritsar District.

                 ,, Ferozepore District.

                 ,, Rawal Pindi District.

                 ,, Bannu District.

                 ,, Peshwar District.

       ,,   ,,   ,, Hazara District.

SHERRING, The Rev. M. A.—Hindu Castes.

VANSITTART, Capt. E.—Notes on Nepal.

FALCON, Capt. R. W.—Handbook of Sikhs.

HUNTER, Sir W. W.—Gazeteer of India.

TOD, Lt.-Col.—Rajasthan.

CUNNINGHAM, J. D.—History of the Sikhs.

Rajputana Gazeteer.

Census Report of Madras, 1891.

                  Bombay, 1891.

     ,,   ,,   Rajputana, 1891.

HODGSON, Mr. B. H.—Notes on the Language, etc., of Nepal.

WRIGHT, Dr.—History of Nepal.

CROOKE, W., B.A., I.C.S. —An Ethnograpical Handbook of the N.-W. P. and Oudh.

THE FIGHTING RACES

OF INDIA.

CHAPTER I.

PATHANS.

THE term Pathan, as commonly used in India, has a
wide and somewhat indefinite application, as it is not in-
frequently used to denote the Pathan proper, the Afghan,
the Tajik, the Hazara, and the Ghilzai. Strictly speaking,
the term is not applicable to the Afghan, Tajik, Hazara or
Ghilzai, who, though they are related to the Pathan proper
by historical, political and geographical association as well
as ethnologically, are nevertheless distinct peoples. The
term can only accurately be applied to certain cognate
peoples of mixed Indian, Afghan, and Scythian origin, who
occupy the Safed Koh, the Suliman and adjacent mountains
with their numerous offshoots, their territorial limits being
bounded, roughly speaking, on the east by the Indus, on
the west by Afghanistan, on the south by Baluchistan, and
on the north by Kashmir and the Kunar River. To
accurately describe the geographical limits of the territory
they occupy would require the mention of many geographical details which do not appear on ordinary maps, and

B, FR   1

hence would not be intelligible to readers unprovided with special maps.

Anything like an accurate and certain account of the ethnology of the Pathan races is not possible, as no very reliable historical data exist. The traditions of the people are vague, conflicting, and misleading, and the only reliable process by which anything like a systematic study and investigation of Pathan ethnology can be undertaken is from their physiological and philological affinities. Pathan tradition ascribes their origin to Jewish sources, the story current among them as well as among the Afghans being that they are the descendants of Saul, the first king of the Jews. The researches of European scholars and ethnologists who have made a critical study of their language, customs, and physical characteristics, would lead to the conclusion that the Pathan is a race closely allied to the Afghan on the one hand, and, though perhaps not so closely, to the certain tribes of Aryan Indians on the other. Indeed, the Pathan can accurately be described as an Indian Afghan, and the probabilities are that they represent the race resulting from the contact of the Afghan with the Indian. Another, and very plausible theory is that the Pathan represents an earlier eastward emigration of certain sections of the same tribes as have given birth to the Afghan. In this view the Pathan and the Afghan are by origin one and the same, the Pathan merely representing an earlier eastward movement of some sections of certain tribes of Jewish or Arab origin, while the Afghan represents the later eastward emigration of other sections of the same tribes.

Whichever view is correct, there can be no doubt but that the Pathan is differentiated from the pure Afghan by possessing certain Indian affinities not possessed by the Afghan. Whether these affinities are due—as probably they are—to an admixture of Indian blood; or whether they are merely the result of close and prolonged political and social contact with India, is of no great practical importance for our purpose. The probabilities are that both Indian blood and Indian surroundings have imparted to the Pathans their Indian affinities.

Mr. D. C. J. Ibbetson of the Indian Civil Service, who has discussed the ethnology of the Punjab races in his Punjab Census Report of 1881, appears to favour the theory that the Pathans are in the main a race of Indian origin; that is, that the Pathan stock is decidedly Indian despite the admixture of foreign blood. According to him, the true Pathans are the modern representatives of an Aryan Indian race styled the Pactiyæ by Herodotus. This race or tribe was subdivided into four great divisions, viz. (1) the Gandhari, who have given birth to the Yusufzai, Mohmund and some other Pathan tribes of the Peshawar District; (2) the Aparytœ, who have evolved into the modern Afridi ; (3) the Satragyaddæ, now known as the Khattaks ; and (4) the Dadicæ or Dadi. This Pactiyan race occupied in the days of Herodotus the mountain country now occupied by the Pathan tribes and constitute the nucleus of these tribes. " Round these tribes as a nucleus have collected many tribes of foreign origin," such as the Jewish or Arab race of Afghans, the Turkish Ghilzai, and the Scythian Kakar ; but all these Indian and foreign tribes have now blended together into one race by intermarriage, intercourse, and close and prolonged association. According to this view the Pathans proper are those Pathan tribes which have a decidedly Pactiyan stock, *i.e.*, those tribes in which the preponderating racial element is Indian, while the mixed Pactiyan and foreign tribes in which the stock is not Indian, but Afghan, Scythian, Turk as the case may be, are Pathan by virtue of their Pactyan blood as well as by their geographical location, association, custom and language.

With this view most will be disposed to agree, the only disputable point being the extent to which each of the component races have participated in the formation of the Pathan. Dr. Bellew, the greatest authority on the subject, and Mr. Ibbetson make the Pathan stock Indian, with an admixture of Afghan and other foreign blood ; whereas officers specially acquainted with the mental and physical characteristics of the Pathans and with their ideas and customs are disposed to the opinion that the stock is in the main Afghan with an admixture of Indian blood. And there is some reason for this opinion. It may be laid down as an axiom that races which are ethnologically one, must, from the very nature of things, when there are no disturbing elements operating, exhibit their ethnic affinity by at least some show of fellow feeling and sympathy. But from the very earliest times that we have any historical records, we find the Pathan arrayed against and despising the Indian. And this antagonism is not merely a practical and political antagonism, but an antagonism of ideals and sentiment. On the other hand, although the Pathan tribes have had constant and bloody feuds with the Afghans and among themselves, in their brief moments of quiescence they display a marked affinity of sentiment, ideals and aims. This seems a very strong argument against the theory of the preponderating Indian origin of the Pathan, as the lapse of a few centuries could scarcely have so completely obliterated their Indian sympathies. While therefore there can be no doubt whatever that there is a considerable admixture of Indian blood in the Pathan, the Pathan stock may be in the main Afghan and not Indian. It is also worthy of remark that the distinctive genius of the Pathan tribes is preponderatingly Afghan and not Indian. Their mental characteristics, ideals and aims approximate much more closely to the Afghan than to any purely Indian tribe we know of.

If the Afghan origin of the Pathan tribes be accepted, it is very probable that they are, as indeed they as all Afghans claim to be, of Jewish origin. Like the Afghans they style themselves Beni-Israel or Children of Israel. There is some evidence in favour of the traditions existing among all Afghan tribes, that they are of Jewish origin, and they may be, as some authorities believe they are, the descendants of the lost tribes of the Jews. Among the evidences in favour of the Jewish origin of the Afghans may be mentioned their close physiological affinity to the Jews, the existence among them of many peculiar social and religious customs which are distinctly Jewish and not Islamic in their origin, and the traditions of the race itself.

According to Afghan traditions they owe their name to their ancestor Afghana, the son of Jeremiah, the son of Saul, the first king of the Jews who was anointed by the Prophet Samuel. This Afghana was reputed to be the Commander of King Solomon's army as well as the designer and builder of his temple. The descendants of Afghana were carried away captive by Nebuchadnezzar to Media and Persia where they bred and multiplied, and gradually increasing, spread over or emigrated to the mountains of Ghor in the tract now known as Afghanistan. Here they remained for several centuries till their conversion to Islam early in the 8th century of our era, under the teaching of one of their tribal leaders Kais or Kish by name, who had married a daughter of Khalid-ibn-walid, a Koreish Arab, who was one of the most enthusiastic of Mahomed's apostles and to whose clan he belonged. Flushed with new life infused by their new faith, and zealous for its propagation, they spread further east into the basin of the Helmund where they found an Indian people, Buddhists by religion, in possession. These people, known as the Gandhari, a tribe of the Pactiyæ of Herodotus, had originally come from the mountains of what is now the Peshawar District, but had been expelled about the 5th century to their new homes about the Helmund by fresh inroads of Scythian invaders from Central Asia. Here they founded a city, Gandhar by name, now known as Kandahar. The Afghans gradually subdued, converted and intermarried with, the Gandhari, adopting their language. There thus came to be two peoples in possession of what is now Southern Afghanistan, namely, the pure Afghans, and a mixed race of Afghans and Gandhari. The pure race came in process of time to become masters of the whole of Afghanistan ; while the mixed race, or considerable portions of it, moved back to the original home of the Gandhari in the Peshawar District, giving rise to the present Yusufzai, Mohmund and certain other Pathan tribes of the Peshawar District.

To sum up, the Pathans may safely be described as a mixed race of partly Afghan, Scythian, Turkish and Persian and partly Indian stock ; the Afghan and other foreign elements preponderating, generally speaking, in those tribes farther away from India and which have not had a very close Indian association, while the Indian element preponderates in those tribes which have had a closer Indian connection.

Of the other races and tribes to which the term Pathan is loosely applied, the Ghilzais are a race of mixed Turkish and Persian descent who have now adopted Pushtoo as their language. The term Ghilzai is a corruption of the Turkish word "Kilchi" which means a swordsman, and the Ghilzais appear to be a tribe of Turkish origin, who emigrating and occupying disputed tracts on the confines of Persia and Afghanistan, gained in process of time an admixture of Persian blood. They appear to have been for centuries a tribe of warlike mercenary soldiers who hired themselves out to fight in the cause of any Chief rich enough to pay them or to hold out hopes of plentiful plunder. They accompanied Mahmud of Ghazni in his invasions of India, and about the 12th century obtained practically independent rule, but under a nominal Persian suzerainty, in the regions about Khelat-i-Ghilzai. They were ultimately reduced to complete subjection by Nadir Shah, the great Persian Emperor, and have now become assimilated with the Afghans by sentiment and association.

The Tajiks, another race to which the term Pathan is applied, are of pure Persian origin, and are supposed to be the remnants of certain Persian tribes who once inhabited Afghanistan before the advent of the Afghans by whom they were subdued. The Tajiks still retain their Persian speech.

The Hazaras are a race of Persian-speaking Tartars who have long settled among the Afghans, but who hold a subordinate and dependent position among them.

There are certain characteristics which are more or less common to all the various Pathan tribes. Like most peoples who have never been accustomed to any form of settled and ordered government, they are a wild, lawless turbulent race, to whom law and order are things to be scoffed at. Further, a people who have never lived under any system of ordered government, must, from the very absence of such government, acquire and develop a strong individualism among its members. For the negation of

law and order which does not provide for the defence
of life and property, but leaves them to be looked after
and guarded by each individual of a community, must
from the very nature of things tend to the formation of
individual self-confidence and self-reliance. And thus it is
that the Pathans are as a race a pre-eminently resolute,
self-reliant people who respect all who can look after
themselves, and despise—very naturally and rightly—those
who have not the grit to hold their own.

The physical features of the country they occupy
have also had a marked effect in the development of the
Pathan character. His wild, bare, gloomy mountains have
imparted to him a certain grim moroseness and sourness
of disposition, which coupled with his strong individualism
make him, though not a very lovable type of humanity,
yet one with some claims to respect and admiration.

As a soldier the Pathan displays great dash and
élan. His passionate nature however, which he has never
been taught to control, soon carries him away, and he is
very apt to lose his head in the heat and frenzy and
excitement of battle. And this leaves him at a disadvantage
as compared with cooler-headed troops who though in
physique his inferior, being in full possession of their
mental faculties and having their emotions well under
control, can fight with greater deliberation and cooler
courage. Bloodthirsty, cruel, revengeful and treacherous,
the Pathan has nevertheless some claims to respect,
for his grit and nerve are things to be proud of ; and if
he is ready to inflict death and reckless in the shedding

of blood, he is generally as reckless of his own life. He takes a just and manly pride in himself, and his resolute look, upright gait, tall and muscular frame, and firm step, betoken many of the qualities of the genuine man.

The fidelity of the Pathan as a soldier has often been doubted, but in the British service he has usually been a loyal and devoted soldier. It would be absurd to expect a high code of honour among a wild and savage people unaccustomed from time immemorial to loyal adhesion to anything in particular. Treachery, often of a cowardly sort, is therefore a common characteristic among them. The Pathan has no sentimental regard and respect for an ideal standard of right, and although he has a code of conduct known as Pakhtunwali, his actions are generally guided by self-interest without any ethical notions of right entering into them. Robbery and murder are as the breath of his nostrils, and his thieving achievements often display an ingenuity worthy of a better cause. Given a rifle, a sufficiency of ammunition, and a wealthy and unprotected traveller or two to operate on, and the Pathan's cup of bliss is full.

Take him for all in all, there is much in him to respect and much to detest. His ideal of a man—and no mean ideal either—is one who is strong, resolute, fearless; and men like John Nicholson, Abbott, Cavagnari, Sandeman, and Battye, endowed with stern integrity of purpose, resolute, inflexible, just, and brave, appeal strongly to the Pathan and could mould the Pathan into a faithful servant of the British Government.

There is a brief description of the Pathan and his
ways given by Mr. Ibbetson in his Census Report which
I quote as being interesting. "The true Pathan is
perhaps the most barbaric of all the races with which
we are brought into contact in the Punjab. His life
is not so primitive as that of the Gipsy tribes. But
he is bloodthirsty, cruel, and vindictive in the highest
degree ; he does not know what truth or faith is,
insomuch that the saying *Afghán be imán* (*i.e.*, an
Afghan is without conscience) has passed into a proverb among his neighbours ; and though he is not
without courage of a sort and is often curiously reckless
of his life, he would scorn to face an enemy whom he
could stab from behind, or to meet him on equal terms
if it were possible to take advantage of him, however
meanly. It is easy to convict him out of his own
mouth ; here are some of his proverbs :—' A Pathan's
enmity smoulders like a dung fire.'—' A cousin's tooth
breaks upon a cousin.'—' Keep a cousin poor but use
him.'—' When he is little play with him ; when he is
grown up, he is a cousin, fight him.'—' Speak good
words to an enemy very softly : gradually destroy him
root and branch.' At the same time he has a code of
honour which he strictly observes, and which he quotes
with pride under the name of Pakhtunwali. It im-
poses on him three chief obligations, *Nanawatai*, or
the right of asylum, which compels him to shelter
and protect even an enemy who comes as a suppliant ;
badal, or the necessity of revenge by retaliation ; and

melmastia, or open-handed hospitality to all who may
demand it. And of these three perhaps the last is
the greatest. And there is a charm about him, especially about the leading men, which almost makes one
forget his treacherous nature. As the proverb says—
' The Pathan is one moment a saint, and the next a
devil.' For centuries he has been, on our frontier at least,
subject to no man. He leads a wild, free, active life in
the rugged fastnesses of his mountains ; and there is an
air of masculine independence about him which is refresh-
ing in a country like India. He is a bigot of the most
fanatical type, exceedingly proud and extraordinarily
superstitious. He is of stalwart make, and his features are
often of a markedly semitic type. His national arms
are the long heavy Afghan knife and the matchlock or
jazail.

"Such is the Pathan in his home among the fastnesses of the frontier ranges. But the Pathans of our
territory have been much softened by our rule and by
the agricultural life of the plains, so that they look down
upon the Pathans of the hills. The nearer he is to the
frontier, the more closely he assimilates to the original
type ; while on this side of the Indus there is little or
nothing, not even language, to distinguish him from his
neighbours of the same religion as himself. The Pathans
are extraordinarily jealous of female honour, and most of
the blood feuds for which they are so famous originate in
quarrels about women. As a race they strictly seclude
their females, but the poorer tribes and the poorer

members of all tribes are prevented from doing so by their poverty. Among the tribes of our territory a woman's nose is cut off, if she be detected in adultery. They intermarry very closely, avoiding only the prohibited degrees of Islam. Their rules of inheritance are tribal and not Mahomedan, and tend to keep property within the agnatic society."

According to the last Census about one million Pathans of all classes are resident in the Punjab within our frontiers, mostly in the districts of Tonk, Marwat, Bannu, Teri, Hangu, Kohat, Peshawar, Nowshera, Doaba, Hashtnagar, Mardan and Utmanbolak. Of the number resident outside our frontier, no reliable information can of course be obtained, but they must number about another million. The population of each tribe is given as far as possible in the description of each which follows.

The language of the Pathan is called Pushtu or Pakhtoo according as it is the soft Persian-influenced dialect, or the hard dialect spoken about Peshawar. Pathan means a speaker of Pushtu. It is an Aryan language bearing a close philological affinity to Persian on the one hand, and to certain early Indian dialects like the Prakrit, on the other. It is thus a mixed language of partly Persian and partly Indian origin. As has already been said, there are two forms of the language as now spoken, *viz.*, Pakhtoo or the Peshwari dialect, which is hard and guttural, and the Pashtoo or Kandahari, which is soft like the Persian, and which is spoken, generally speaking, by the tribes living on the south-west who have had a larger Persian connection than their northern and eastern brethren.

It was probably not till the 14th century that Pushtu finally blossomed into the full dignity of a written language. Previous to that time there was no written literature in the language. The race has however, improved in intellectuality since then, as they have produced a few authors like the Yusufzai historian Shaikh Mali, who flourished in the 15th century ; the Khattak poet, warrior and chief, Khushal Khan, who flourished during the 17th century, and whose poems have gained for him the designation of the "Father of Afghan Poetry" ; Abdul Hamid, the Mohmund poet, and others. Such books as there are in the language are mostly historical and biographical records of the various tribes, poetical effusions of sorts —though some like those of Khushal Khan are of great merit—and religious tracts.

The Pathan territories occupy several thousand square miles of mountainous country partly within and partly without our frontier from as far south as Baluchistan to the Hindukhush on the north and Kashmir on the north-east. Through these mountains, whose elevation varies from 3,000 to 8,000 feet, flow the Gomal, the Kurram, the Zhob, the Kabul and other smaller rivers with their tributaries. The principal tributaries of the Kabul River are the Chitral, the Bara, the Swat, and the Kalpani Rivers. The rainfall in this region is scanty and uncertain, and agricultural operations can only be carried on properly in those tracts watered and fertilised by the rivers mentioned.

The Pathan tribes are partly agricultural and partly nomad pastorals. Their migrations are, however, on a small and restricted scale, being merely annual moves within their own areas from one grazing ground to another ; or from the hot valleys to the cool retreats of the higher mountain ranges in the summer, and from the snowclad mountain heights to the lower and warmer regions in winter. They live mostly in substantial villages which for comfort compare favourably with an ordinary Indian village. Their houses are roughly built structures of stone and slate which abound in their native hills, plastered with earth. Their houses are often surrounded by small flower and fruit gardens which give them an appearance of comfort not observable in an Indian homestead. Squalor and filth are inevitable accompaniments of all Oriental villages, but on the whole the Pathan is better housed and fed than one would expect from so poor a people. In addition to their agricultural and pastoral pursuits, a large number of Pathans of each tribe obtain their livelihood as petty merchants or traders, carrying goods in caravans between India, Afghanistan and Central Asia. These wandering traders are called Powindahs, a term derived from the Persian word Parwindah, which signifies a bale of goods. Forming large and well-armed caravans they are the chief means of carrying English manufactures to Afghanistan and Central Asia, and as such enjoy an important economic position.

Pathan villages are divided into several distinct allotments or subdivisions called *Kandis*, according to the number of subdivisions of the tribe residing in it. Thus in each village each group of families which goes to form a *Khel* or clan has each its own Kandi, at the head of which is a *malik* or elder who acts as its judge, manager, and administrator. In each Kandi again there is a *jamaat* or mosque under a *mullah* or priest ; an assembly room called *hujra*, where its residents meet to discuss their affairs, and where visitors and travellers can claim shelter ; and in transfrontier villages where life and property are never safe, a watch tower and citadel for defence purposes known as a *burj*. At the head of each tribe is a Chief styled *Khan*, to whom the maliks are subordinate. Being intensely independent and impatient of control, it is not surprising that neither maliks nor Khans enjoy any real powers. As Mr. Ibbetson puts it, they possess influence rather than power. All matters of general tribal interest are settled by the decision of a *jirgah* or council of maliks, in which the real controlling authority resides, the Khan or tribal Chief merely acting as president of the tribal *jirgah*, as their leader in times of war, and in times of peace their accredited agent for inter-tribal communication.

Among a rude, untamed, independent race like the Pathan, impatient of all restraint, there can be very little like ordered government, and as a matter of fact the several clans and septs decide their disputes independently of any central controlling authority. The various tribes form so many antagonistic commonwealths under the presidency of their Khans, perpetually at war with one another, and when not warring against one another, torn by internal disputes and feuds among themselves. The office of malik and Khan are generally hereditary except in cases where the hereditary claimant shews palpable evidence of physical or mental incapacity, in which case there is nothing to prevent any man of ability and courage being elected to either office.

The great majority of the Pathan tribes are Sunni Mahomedans of a bigoted sort, the exceptions being the Turis and some of the Bangash and Orakzai clans who are Shiahs.

As has already been stated, there are five distinct races to the fusion of two or more of which the various Pathan tribes owe their origin. These races are :—

    (1) An Aryan race styled the Pactyæ by Herodotus.
    (2) The Afghan, a race of mixed Jewish and Arab origin.
    (3) The Persian.
    (4) The Scythian or Tartar.
    (5) The Turk.

In some tribes, which constitute the Pathan tribes proper, the ethnic stock—that is, the preponderating racial element—is Indian or Pactyan with an admixture of either Afghan, Persian, Scythian or Turkish blood. In other tribes the stock is Afghan with an admixture of Indian blood. In others again the stock is Persian with an admixture of Indian or other blood ; and so on. Hence all the Pathan tribes can be classified according as their ethnic stock is Indian, Afghan, Persian, Scythian or Turkish.

This basis of division cannot, however, be adopted for practical purposes, as the classification which would thus be obtained would not correspond exactly to the existing traditional classification among the various tribes which is based on a common descent from the three sons of Kais or Kish, who was in his turn a reputed descendant of Saul, first king of the Jews. There are a large number of Pathan tribes, and these are again subdivided into a bewildering number of clans, sub-clans and septs. Confusion is made worse by many of the subdivisions of the several tribes bearing the same name. For example, "Utmanzai" is a name borne by a clan of Mandaner Yusufzais, by a clan of Bar or transfrontier Mohmunds, and by a clan of Darwesh Khel Waziris. Again, the name "Alizai" is borne by a clan of the Daudzai tribe as well as by a clan of Turis. It is therefore necessary in the case of clans having the same name to specify the tribe to which they belong.

The three sons of Kais or Kish, from whom the various tribes claim a common descent, were Sarban, Gurghusht and Baitan, and the Pathan and Afghan tribes classify themselves according as they are the progeny of one or other of these sons; the descendants of Sarban being known as Sarbanni Pathans, those of Gurghusht as Gurghushti Pathans, and those of Baitan as the Baitanni Pathans.

In order to shew clearly the ethnic as well as the traditional classification of the Pathans I give below two tables shewing both :—

ETHNOLOGICAL CLASSIFICATION.

Tribes of Pactyan or Indian stock.

(1) Waziris.
(2) Bannuchis.
(3) Dawris.
(4) Tane.
(5) Khattak.
(6) Afridi.
(7) Utman Khel.
(8) Jadran.

(9) Bangash.
(10) Orakzai.
(11) Dilazak.
(12) Hanni.
(13) Wardag.
(14) Mangal.
(15) Bitanni.

Tribes of Afghan stock.

(1) Muhammadzai.
(2) Shinwari.
(3) Yusufzai.
(4) Tarklanri.
(5) Surgiani.
(6) Mullagori (doubtful. Perhaps Indian.)

(7) Mohmund.
(8) Daudzai.
(9) Khalil.
(10) Chamkani or Chakmani.
(11) Zirani.

Tribes of Scythian stock.

(1) Kakar.
(2) Ushtarani.

(3) Bakhtiar.
(4) Shirani.

Tribes of pure Afghan stock.

(1) Abdalli or Duranni.
(2) Tarin.

(3) Miana.
(4) Baraich.

Tribes of mixed Turkish and Afghan stock.

(1) Khugianni.
(2) The Ghilzai tribes, *viz.*—

    (*a*) Hotak.
    (*b*) Kharoti.
    (*c*) Tokhi.
    (*d*) Nasar.

} known as Turan Pathans.

  (e) Suleman Khel.
  (f) Ali Khel.
  (g) Akha Khel.
  (h) Ishaq.   }known as Ibrahimzais.
  (i) Andar.
  (f) Tarakki.

(3) The Lodi tribes, viz.—

  (a) Dutanni.
  (b) Naizi or Niazai.
  (c) Sur.
  (d) Prangi.
  (e) Sarwani.
  (f) Khasor.
  (g) Marwat.
  (h) Mian Khel.
  (i) Daulat Khel. }known as Lohani Pathans.
  (j) Tator.

  The uncertainty which attaches to Pathan ethnology renders it impossible for an absolutely accurate classification based on racial affinity, but the above will be found sufficiently accurate for all practical purposes. For recruiting purposes the table opposite, giving the traditional classification existing among the tribes, will also be found useful.

  In order to understand the table it is necessary to remark that Kharshabun and Sharkabun were the two sons of Sarbun, the three sons of the former being named Kand, Zamand and Kansi. Karlan, after whom the Karlanri tribes are named, was a descendant of Gurghusht. Baitan's descent in the male line are now known as the Bitanni. Through his daughter Bibi Matto,

however, who was married to a fugitive Persian prince
Shah Hussain by name, Baitan has become the progenitor
of a large number of tribes who are collectively known
as the Matti Pathans.

I proceed now to give a descriptive sketch of the more
important Pathan tribes.

Afridis.—The Afridis, one of the most important and
powerful of the Pathan tribes, number in all about
250,000 souls, of whom some 15,000 are resident within
our frontier. They could on an emergency muster
about 30,000 well-armed fighting men. They occupy
so much of the Safed Koh range as lies immediately
south and west of the Peshawar District, their northern
limit being somewhat below the Kabul River and
their southern the Kohat District. The territory they
occupy is in extent about 900 square miles. The plateau
known as Tirah is shared by them with the Orakzai.
They have as their neighbours the Mohmunds on the
north, the Orakzais on the south, and the Shinwaris on
the west. They claim to be, like all Pathans, of Jewish
origin, but the probabilities are that they are a tribe of
Pactyan stock with an admixture of Turkish or Scythian
blood. Living as they do on the high road from Central
Asia to India, *via* the Khaiber Pass, it is probable that
they have a large admixture of Central Asian, that is,
Turkish and Scythian, blood in them. Their country
being bleak and sterile, and generally rainless, does not
afford much scope for agricultural operations, and the
wealth of the people therefore, such as it is, consists of

their flocks and herds, mostly sheep and goats. Like most pastoral peoples who are either unacquainted with or averse to the tedious labour of settled agriculture, they are a wild race of hardy nomads. Their migrations are, however, restricted in character, being but an annual move during the hot months to the cool higher slopes of Tirah and during winter when the higher regions are covered with snow, to the lower valleys of the Bazar and Bara rivers.

Agriculture is however, not entirly unknown among them as they succeed in raising a coarse species of rice in the river valleys where the presence of a water-supply enables them to carry on agricultural operations. Some of the tribe also gain a scanty livelihood by cutting and selling for firewood the timber which abounds in their hills. They also go in for breeding horses, donkeys and mules, which they turn out of a fairly good quality.

There are eight great clans among the Afridis, *viz.* —

(1) Akha Khel.	(5) Kambar Khel.
(2) Adam Khel.	(6) Malik Din Khel.
(3) Zaka Khel.	(7) Kamar Khel or
(4) Sipah.	Kumarai.

(8) The Kuki Khel.

Of these clans the last six are collectively known as the Khaiber Afridis and claim a common descent from one Ula, a son of Afrid, the founder and progenitor of the whole tribe.

The holdings of the Khaiber Afridis abut on the Khaiber Pass. The Akha Khel occupy the mountains south of the Bara River, while the Adam Khel have their holdings in the mountains between the Kohat and Peshawar Districts.

The Jowaki Afridis against whom some punitive expeditions have from time to time been sent are a sept of the Adam Khel clan.

The Afridis, who supply a large number of soldiers to our frontier Native regiments, possess in an eminent degree the dash and élan which more or less characterise all the Pathan tribes. They are physically fine types of men, being tall, hardy, muscular, and able to endure protracted exposure and hardship. Brave, fearless, ready to meet as to inflict death, the Afridi is morose, bloodthirsty, cruel, and has the reputation, perhaps undeservedly, of possessing to a pre-eminent degree the besetting sin of all Pathans, treachery. Proud, resolute, and self-reliant, he makes an ideal soldier for our Native army.

Yusufzais.—The Yusufzais are perhaps the largest, and are certainly one of the most important and powerful of the Pathan tribes. They are a race of Afghan stock with a Gandharian admixture. Their settlements and holdings occupy a large tract of plain and mountainous country north and east of the Peshawar District as well as considerable tracts of plain country in the Peshawar District itself. They claim a Jewish origin, and their traditions place their original home in the mountain fastnesses of Khorossan, from whence they were gradually driven to their present holdings.

The tribe is divided into two great branches, *viz.*, the Yusufzai proper and the Mandaner. Both these branches claim a common descent from one Mandai. This Mandai had two sons, Yusuf and Umar. The Yusufzai proper trace their descent to Yusuf, while the Mandaner claim to be descended from Mandan, the son of Umar. Both these two branches have settlements partly within and partly without our frontier ; but broadly speaking the Yusufzais proper are in the main a transfrontier people occupying the hill country known as Buner, Swat and their sur-roundings ; while the Mandaner are mainly a cis-frontier people occupying the tashils of Mardan and Swabi in the Peshawar District, portions of territory in the Hazara Mountains and parts of the Chamla Valley.

The Yusufzai proper are divided into five main clans known as a Isazai, the Iliazai, the Malizai, the Ranizai and the Akozai ; while the Mandaner have three great subdivisions, namely, the Usmanzais, the Utmanzai and the Razar.

Yusufzais, whether Mandaner or Yusufzai proper, are very often known by their geographical situation as Bunerwals, Swatis, Chamlawals, &c., that is, as the inha-bitants of the tracts known as Buner, Swat, Chamla, &c.

The tribe is in the main agricultural, but the Yusufzais are also largely possessed of flocks and herds. They were originally a race of nomad pastorals, but have now settled down into fixed agricultural and pastoral pursuits. They make capital soldiers and possess all the virtues and all the vices common to the Pathan race.

It is impossible to say exactly what the population of the tribe is, but 300,000 may be taken as a sufficiently close approximation. Of these, the last Census shewed 121,000 as residing within our border.

Bangash.—The Bangashes, who occupy the north-western parts of the Kohat District and some adjacent tracts in the Kurram Valley, are probably a tribe of Indian origin with a large Scythian admixture. Their own traditions, however, claim for them an Arab origin. Dr. Bellew is inclined to think that they are in the main of Scythian origin, and that they came into India with the Scythic hordes of Central Asia which accompanied Sabaktagin and Timur. They have occupied their present holdings for several centuries, and about the 15th and 16th centuries appear to have been a tribe of some historical importance. One of the early Chiefs of the tribe, Ismail by name, who lived about the 14th century, was Governor of Multan and was a man of much local importance in his day and generation. He had two sons, named Gar and Samil, whose mutual quarrels and jealousies led the tribe being split up into two great factions which still exist, and known after the brother each sided with as the Gar and the Samil factions. It would appear that the brothers enlisted the sympathies of some of the other Pathan tribes so that the Gar and Samil factions are not restricted to the Bangashes alone, but extend to all the other Pathan tribes who were mixed up in the feuds of the two brothers.

The term Bangash means " root-destroyer," and the term came to be applied as the tribal name because of the cruel oppressions of Ismail and his two sons.

The tribe is divided into four main clans known as the Miranzai, the Samilzai, the Jamshedis and the Baizai. The Bangashes are on the whole of very fair physique, the Baizai clan especially being a well-set-up body of people, fair and good-looking. They are very ignorant, superstitious and bigoted, and though not possessing such a high reputation for courage as some other Pathan tribes, such as there are in our Native army, have made very good soldiers.

Khattaks.—The Khattaks are an exceedingly fine race, brave, faithful, and for Pathans, truthful and honest. Ethnologically, they are like the Bangashes, of Indian stock with a Scythian admixture. It will be noticed from the genealogical table that the Khattaks are a Karlanri tribe, being descended from Karlan through his son Kakai, grandson Burhan, and great grandson Lokhman. They are thus, traditionally at least, closely related to the Afridi. They occupy a semi-circular tract of country, embracing the north-east of the Bannu District, the whole eastern portions of the Kohat District and the south-east corner of the Peshawar District. They are thus wholly within our borders. They are numerically only a small tribe numbering according to the last Census about 120,000 souls, but have some pretensions to historical importance as they were entrusted by Akbar with the duty of guarding the road to Peshawar, in return for certain grants of land. The Khattak Chiefs were thus recognised by the Mogul Emperors, and for some time they were their accredited agents for the protection of the Khaiber border.

They also rendered from time to time considerable military services to the Delhi Emperors, although their great Chief Khushal Khan rebelled against Aurangzebe. The tribe has produced several men of great ability, and in intellectuality the tribe is much ahead of other Pathan tribes. Khushal Khan was not only a great warrior and Chief, but as has already been mentioned he enjoys a very considerable reputation as a poet. His grandson Afzal Khan is also known to fame as a poet. Another of their great men was their saint Rahim Kar, whose grave near Nowshera is still the resort of many pilgrims.

The tribal subdivisions of the Khattak are very perplexing. They make excellent material for our Native army, being more amenable to discipline, more trustworthy and more intelligent than most Pathans. They are brave and industrious, make excellent horsemen, and altogether the Pathan is seen at his best in the Khattak. The only drawback is the numerical paucity of the tribe, which restricts the supply of soldiers. The country they occupy is generally sterile, but they manage by steady industry to raise some crops, but they also possess large flocks and herds, and carry on a large trade as carriers and vendors of salt and fuel.

Mohmunds.—This tribe belongs to the Ghoria Khel section of the Sarbanni Pathans. Their Chief is styled *Arbab* or lord, in contradistinction to most other Pathan tribes whose Chiefs are styled Khans. Ethnologically they are of Afghan stock, but the unhealthiness of some of the tracts they occupy has made certain sections of the tribe of inferior physique to the generality of the Afghan races. Their holdings occupy several hundred square miles of hill and plain country partly within our frontier in the Peshawar District and partly without our boundaries in the hills immediately north and west of that district. They have as their neighbours, on the east the great Yusufzai tribe ; on the north, the Utmankhels and Tarklanris or Bajouris as they are often called ; on the west, the Daudzais ; and on the south, the Orakzai. The southern limit of their territory is the Kabul River. Their fighting strength is about 19,000.

The Mohmunds are divided into two main branches, the Kuz or plains Mohmunds who are as a whole within our frontier, and the Bar or transfrontier hill Mohmunds who are independent. There is little or no cohesion or sympathy between these two great branches of the tribe, and for all practical purposes they are distinct peoples. Owing to their territories being fairly well watered, the Mohmunds have now settled down into a tribe of agriculturists and succeed in raising sufficient crops for their support. The Kuz Mohmunds are men of good physique, but their Bar brethren as a whole do not compare favourably either in physique or in warlike characteristics with other Afghan tribes.

The Kuz branch is divided into five classes, viz., the Mayarzai, the Musazai, the Dawezai, the Mattanni, and the Sirgani. The Bar Mohmunds have seven main divisions among themselves, viz., the Baizai, the Dawezai, the Halimzai, the Utmanzai, the Khwaizai, the Kukuzai, and the Tarakzai.

There are very few of the tribe in our Native army, there being no great demand for them, as the Mohmund clans excepting a few have not got a high reputation for courage, although they display all the violence of the Pathans in their dealings with one another.

Waziris.—Dr. Bellew and Mr. Ibbetson are inclined to think that the Waziris are a tribe of Rajput origin. Their own traditions represent them to be the descendants of Wazir, the son of Suleiman, the son of Kakai, the son of Karlan, so that they are a tribe of Karlanri Pathans. It is probable that they are ethnologically a race of Indian origin with a large admixture of Scythian or Tartar blood. The Waziri territory lies partly within but mostly without British limits and in the main immediately west of the Kohat and Bannu Districts. Their northern limit may, roughly speaking, be taken as a line drawn almost due west through Thull in the Bungash country, and their extreme southern limit a line drawn due west of Dera Fateh Khan. Practically however, the majority of Waziri settlements are not further south than the Gomal River.

The Waziris are a large and powerful tribe and are divided into four great clans, *viz.*, the Darwesh Khel, the Gurbaz, the Mahsud, and the Lali. Of these the Darwesh Khel and the Mahsud are the most important and powerful, the other two being small clans and not of much political or military importance. The Darwesh Khel are again divided into two sub-clans, the Ahmadzai

and the Utmanzai. The connection between the several
clans is as follows. Sulaiman, the progenitor of the tribe,
had two sons, Lalai and Khizrai. The Lalai clan is descended from Lalai. Khizrai had three sons, Musa Darwesh, Gurbaz, and Mahsud. From Musa Darwesh are
descended the Darwesh Khel clan, and from the other two
sons, the clans now known by their names.

The whole tribe holds a high reputation for courage
and warlike qualities, and being strong, muscular, hardy
men, make excellent fighting material. The restraints of
discipline are, however, specially irksome to them, and
they shew no disposition to enlist. They are cruel and
bloodthirsty to a degree, but enjoy the reputation of
having a higher code of truth, chivalry and fidelity than
other Pathans. Expert in thieving, much of their support is obtained by plundering not only caravans but
also the territories of their neighbours. Their country is
fairly well watered, enabling them to raise some crops,
but the steady and patient industry required for agriculture is burdensome to them so that they subsist largely
on their flocks and herds. On the whole, the Waziris are
a tribe possessing much manly independence and backbone and are in many respects a fine race. Their attack
on our camp at Wana in the autumn of 1894 is justly
admired for its resolute courage.

Orakzais.—The Orakzais are a nomad Pathan tribe
inhabiting the hills south-west of the Peshawar District,
and north of the Kohat District. Their territories, which
lie partly in the tract known as Tirah, are alongside the

Afridi Hills. They are a fairly large tribe, subdivided into a great many smaller clans and septs between whom there is very little cohesion. Their fighting strength is about 15,000 men. Their main divisions are five, namely, the Masuzai or Masozai, the Ismailzai, the Daulatzai, the Alizai and the Lashkarzai. In physique the Orakzais do not compare favourably with either the Waziri or the Afridi, but they are nevertheless hardy and strong men, enured to fatigue and exposure. In other respects they are much like other Pathans. Their chief source of wealth lies in their flocks and herds, but they also go in largely for mule and donkey breeding. The Daulatzai and Masozai are the most numerous of their clans.

Shinwaris.—This tribe is in the main agricultural, as the tracts they occupy are well watered, fertile, and productive. Wheat, barley, rice and various kinds of fruit, such as the apple, peach, pomegranate, are raised in sufficiently large quantities to admit of a small export to Peshawar and the neighbouring cantonments. The eastern Shinwari tracts are not, however, so fertile as the rest, and hence some of its inhabitants earn their livelihood as carriers, wood-cutters and by other manual pursuits. The Shinwaris are a tribe of Afghan stock, and their country lies north of the Khaiber Pass, south of the Khugianni country and east of the Mullagoris. They are divided into the Sangu Khel, the Mandozai or Manduzai, the Sipah and the Ali Sher Khel clans. The tribe is not large numerically or of much political importance, but they are brave men and make capital soldiers. Liv-

ing among the Sangu Khel is a clan of Ghilzais known
as the Mir Jan Khel, who have now become thoroughly
naturalised Shinwaris.

Turis.—The Turis, or Torizais as they are sometimes
called, are ethnologically a tribe of mixed blood, being
of Indian stock with a Tartar admixture.   Mr. Ibbetson
regards them as being probably Tartar tribes which
accompanied Changiz and Taimur in their Indian raids.
Their own traditions make them out to be of Duranni
or Abdalli, that is of pure Afghan, origin, and there is
some evidence in favour of this claim.   The Turis occupy
the Kurram, and are a fine race, being muscular, wiry
and brave.   Their traditions have it that some six centuries ago the tribe emigrated into the Kurram from the
Punjab, and that at first they dwelt among the Bungashes
as hamsayas or vassals, occupying a subordinate and
dependent position among them.   Owing to Bungash
emigration eastward, the Turis gradually absorbed the
remnants of the Bungash, and thus ultimately acquired
the chief position in Kurram.   The Turis are divided into
five clans, the Alizai, the Duparzai and the Gundi Khel,
which are collectively known as the Chardai ; and the
Mastu Khel and Hamza Khel, which are grouped together
and known as the Sargalli section.

The tribe is not a large one numerically, and the
recently raised Kurram Militia, to which is entrusted the
duty of guarding the Kurram border, and which consists
mainly of Turis, furnishes a convenient organisation which
may be increased, but not to any large extent.

Zaimukht or Zaimusht.—The Zaimukht are a tribe of Afghan stock inhabiting the Kurram, adjoining the Turis and west of the Kohat border. Their eastern neighbours are the Bangash, and their northern the Orakzai and Afridi. They are strong, powerful, well-built men, of pleasing features, and are brave and warlike. They are in the main agriculturists, but their chief source of income is derived from the tolls they levy for the safe conduct of the caravans using the main trade route through the Peiwar Kotal. The tribe is divided into the Mamozai or Muhammadzai and the Koidad Khel sections.

Bajouris or Tarklanris.—The Bajouris are the people inhabiting Bajour, a tract of mountainous country lying north of the Utman Khel and Mohmund country. Within this area, several distinct Pathan tribes are located, but the most numerous and powerful are the Tarkanis or Tarklanris, an Afghan (or perhaps Tartar or Turki) race possessing considerable reputation for courage and intelligence. The Bajour country was originally in possession of the Gujars, a race of purely Indian origin, whom the Tarkanis subjugated and dispossessed, and small colonies of whom still live in dependence on them. Other tribes resident in Bajour are considerable numbers of Yusufzais, Shinwaris, Dehgans, which have been sketched in their proper places.

The Tarkanis are physically a grand race of men, tall and fair-complexioned, and with finely cut features. They are intelligent and industrious, and being hardy, muscular and brave, make very good fighting material. Rice, wheat and barley are extensively grown in Bajour, and the people are also largely possessed of flocks and herds.

Kakars.—The Kakars are in the main a tribe of Scythian stock, but they have now absorbed into themselves several clans of Rajput and Indian origin. Dr. Bellew thinks they are of the same race as the Ghakkars. There are six main clans among them known as the Babé Khel, the Dadi or Kundi, the Kakar proper, the Mandu Khel, the Panni, and the Nagar. Of these, the Kakar proper probably represents that section of the Scythian stock which has maintained its purity of blood with a minimum of Indian admixture. The Dadi or Kundi are according to Mr. Ibbetson the modern representatives of the Dadi of Herodotus, to whom reference has been made before ; while, according to the same authority, the Panni and Nagar are supposed to be of Rajput origin. The Kakars have their holdings in the Zhob Valley and on either side of the Bori River, south of the extreme southern limit of the Waziris. They are not very numerous, but make good soldiers.

Minor Pathan Tribes.—Of the lesser Pathan tribes, a very brief description must suffice. The *Ghigianis or Gugianis* are an Afghan tribe living north-west of Peshawar between the junction of the Swat and Kabul Rivers. They are a small and unimportant tribe, somewhat despised by their more powerful neighbours, and neither in physique or in valour do they come up to the standard of the better Pathan tribes. The *Degans or*

Dehgans are supposed to be a tribe either of Hindu origin, or to have come from Kaffiristan. They embraced Islam several centuries ago and are now found mostly about Jelalabad. They are of no importance either politically or for military purposes. The *Daudzais* are an Afghan tribe living about the Kabul River between the Mohmunds and the Gugianis. They are of rather poor physique as their country is malarious and unhealthy. The *Khalils*, though numerically a small tribe, are a brave race of men, and are of Afghan stock. Their settlements lie along that of the Mohmunds. Their clans are four in number : the Barozai, the most important ; the Ishaqzai, the Matuzai and the Tillarzai. Plunder is their chief source of livelihood, but they are glad to enlist in our Native army. The *Marwats*, who live within our borders in the Bannu District, are Ghilzais by descent and make capital soldiers. They are a handsome race, fair, tall and broad. They make good agriculturists, but the tribe is mainly pastoral. The *Muhammadzais*, who live in the Hashtnagar tashil in the north-west of the Peshawar District, are a brave but small tribe of Afghan stock. The *Mullagoris*, whose holdings are immediately north of the Afridis, are a small thieving tribe of probably Indian descent. They are despised by other Pathan tribes, who deny them the distinction of being Pathans at all. The *Niazais or Niazi*, who live in the Bannu District alongside of the Marwat, are like the Marwat of Ghilzai descent. They were some centuries back a very important tribe, and are still numerically pretty large. The last Census shews the Niazai population at 640,000, but this is probably an overestimate. They are not industrious, but make good soldiers. They have an evil reputation for lawlessness. The *Tirahis* are a small Afghan tribe of agriculturists living about Jelalabad. The *Safis and Shaonkanris* are insignificant tribes living about Jelalabad and the Safed Koh. The former are supposed to be of Kafir origin. The *Chakmanis or Chamkanis* are a small tribe of Afghan origin living immediately south of the Safed Koh, and east of the Turis. The *Ushteranis*, who live to the south of Dera Ismail Khan, occupy a part of the Suleiman Mountains. They are probably a race of Scythian stock with an Arab admixture. They are a fine tribe, manly, industrious, and brave. The *Shiranis* are an Afghan tribe occupying the tracts around the Takht-i-Suleiman mountain, north of the Ushteranis. They have a considerable admixture of Kakar blood. They are a wild and hardy tribe who would make good soldiers. The *Bitannis* are an Afghan tribe occupying the frontier between Bannu and Tonk. The *Turin* Pathans occupy the mountains about Peshin and Thal Chotiali. They are in the main of Afghan stock. The *Dawris* are the tribe inhabiting the Tochi Valley off the Bannu border. The Tochi river waters their country. They are not held in much repute. The *Bannuchis*, who occupy portions of the Bannu District, are one of the worst Pathan tribes, being a depraved race of criminals, and without any of the instincts of the genuine soldier. The *Khetrans* are partly Pathan and partly Baluch, occupying portions of land off the Baluch frontier. They are not very warlike.

As has already been said, there are certain tribes which by location and association are commonly styled Pathans, but are not so in reality. Of these, the Hazaras and Tajiks have already been briefly referred to. Of the other tribes of so-called Pathans, the *Tanaolis or Tanawalis* claim a Mogul origin, but are in reality a tribe of Aryan Indians. Their holdings are in Tanawal on the Hazara border, and they are divided into two great sections, the Hindwal and the Pallal. They make good agriculturists, but are not very warlike. The *Gaduns or Jaduns* like the Tanaolis call themselves Pathan and claim to be of Gurghushti origin. The probabilities are they are of Rajput origin. Their settlements are mostly in Hazara, and they have three main sections among themselves, the Salar, Mansur and Hassazai.

Reference has been made to the two political factions known as the Samil and Gar, which exist among certain of the tribes. The traditional explanation for the existence of these two factions has been given above. Dr. Bellew is, however, of opinion that the ultimate origin of the two factions is traceable much further back, to the times before the conversion of the Pathan tribes to Muhammadanism, when they were partly Buddhistic and partly Magian in their religious beliefs. According to this view the Samil and Gar factions owe their origin to the original religious division of the people into Buddhists, and followers of the early Zoroastrian religion of Persia.

Whatever the origin of these two factions, time has not healed the bitterness and animosity between them, and even now bloody feuds are not uncommon between the factions. The following tribes and sections of tribes belong to the Samil faction,—the whole of the Mohmund tribe, the Akha Khel, the Adam Khel, the Zaka Khel, Sipah, Malik Din Khel, and Kamar Khel clans of the Afridi tribes, half of the Bangash, and half the Orakzai. The Gar faction comprises the other half of the Bangash and Orakzai tribes, the Kuki Khel and Kamar Khel Afridis, and the Khalil.

CHAPTER II.

BALUCHIS.

BALUCHISTAN, the land of the Baluchis and Brahuis, is bounded on the north by Afghanistan, on the east by Sind and the Punjab, on the south by the Arabian Sea, and on the west by Persia. The western boundary is however, somewhat indefinite, but, roughly speaking, may be taken as a line drawn due north of Gwetter or Gwadr Bay on the Arabian Sea, the only deviation being a bend east and then back west about the centre of this line. The greatest length of the country is about 550 miles and its greatest breadth 370 miles, the total area being about 161,000 square miles. It is generally hilly and in parts mountainous, but the elevation rarely exceeds 11,000 feet, the highest elevation being that of Chehil Tan, a peak in the Herbui range of mountains which rises to a height of 12,000 feet above sea-level. Towards the north-east and east the mountains attain very respectable proportions, but dwindle down considerably towards the south and west. The principal mountain systems are (1) the Herbui, Khirtari, and Hala Mountains on the north and east; (2) the Durram, Talar and Hingor Hills, on the south running parallel to the south coast at some distance from it; (3) the Kohek, Sarband and Nehbandan Mountains running east and west across the western boundary; (4) the Wusuti or

Mue Mountains forming part of the northern boundary between Afghanistan and Baluchistan ; (5) the Sarawani Mountains running in a north-easterly direction in the western districts ; and (6) the Bashkhird Mountains.

Baluchistan is divided into seven provinces or divisions, viz., Kachh-Gandava in the north-east ; Jhalawan in the centre and east ; Sarawan in the north ; Lus or Luz, sometimes also called Bela, on the south-eastern coast ; Mekran on the south-western coast ; Kohistan on the west ; and Khelat in the centre.

As a whole the country is rugged and arid, and suffers from a deficiency of water, though a fairly plentiful rainfall occurs in February and March. It is therefore in the main sandy, barren and unproductive, but there are tracts, especially in Kachh-Gandava, which are very fertile and capable of producing large crops. Fruit, such as dates, apples, peaches, pomegranates, pistachio nuts and figs, are largely grown ; as also cotton, indigo, tobacco and wheat, but to a smaller extent. Gold, silver and copper are found in parts, but no systematic mining operations are carried on to any appreciable extent, and manufactures are practically non-existent. There are no large rivers, and such as there are lose themselves in the desert sands which abound all over the country. The principal rivers are the Bolan flowing through the north-east of Sarawan and into Kachh-Gandava ; the Lora or Lorashorawak, a tributary of the Helmund, in the north of Sarawan ; the Sirinab also in Sarawan ; the Rodbat in the north ; the Mūla in eastern Khelat and west

Kachh-Gandava ; the Mari in the western part of Kachh-
Gandava ; the Nal in the north-east, a tributary of the
Indus ; the Urnach in south Jhalawan ; the Poorally
flowing south through Lus into the Arabian Sea ; the
Desht or Dasht in Mekran flows in a westerly direction
into the Arabian Sea ; the Dorak or Nal in central Jhalawan ; the Habb, Sinamani and Nari in the east ; the
Rakshan, Gwargo and Nihing in the west. There are in
addition a large number of petty streams. Some of these
rivers are sometimes liable to sudden floods owing to
storms in the higher elevations of the hills in which they
rise.

The principal towns are Khelat, the capital of the
whole country as well as of the province so named ;
Mastung, the capital of Sarawan ; Kozdar, the capital of
Jhalawan ; Bela, of Lus or Bela ; Kej, of Mekran ; and
Bagh, of Kachh-Gandava. Other important towns are
Quetta, Sarawan, Sonmiani, Sohrab, Nushki and Dera.
Dera Ismail Khan, Dera Fatteh Khan and Dera Ghazi
Khan, although now in British territory, were originally
founded by Baluch Chiefs, named Ismail Khan, Fatteh
Khan and Ghazi Khan, the two former being the sons
of Malik Sohrab Khan, one of the early Chiefs of the
Dodai tribe of Baluchis.

The population is about half a million consisting
mainly of Baluchis and Brahuis, but with a large preponderance of the former. Both these two races, which are
ethnologically distinct, are mainly pastoral and to a great
extent nomad. The Baluchis speak a dialect of Persian

origin and are tall, oval-featured men; while the Brahuis, who are the dominant race in the country, are thick-set, flat-featured men, comparatively short of stature, but strong, muscular and hardy, whose language appears to have an Indian affinity, though some authorities maintain it is of Iranian origin.

The Baluchis claim to be a race of Arab stock, their traditions ascribing their origin to Hamzah, an Arab of the Koreish tribe to which the Prophet Mahomed belonged. Hamzah himself, the traditional progenitor of the race, was the uncle of Mahomed. The theory of the Koreish origin of the race is probably a pure fiction which has been invented owing to the natural desire of all Mahomedan peoples to claim a more or less close connection with their Prophet ; but there is sufficient evidence in favour of the general tradition existing among Baluchis of their Arab origin. Their physiological affinities closely approximate to the Arab, and there is enough evidence extant shewing that they were a people who emigrated into their present territories from the direction of Arabia.

Hamzah, the traditional progenitor of the race, was, in his day, one of the most important of the early Mahomedan Chiefs. A great warrior, a man of extraordinary personal strength and courage, he was fitly styled the Lion of God. Hamzah was killed at the Battle of Ohod in the year 625 A.D. His descendants and adherents, according to Baluch tradition, settled about Aleppo in the north of Syria, from where they were expelled by Yezid, son and successor of Muavia, the first Omeyeid Caliph. The reason for this expulsion was the assistance which the adherents of Hamzah had given to Hossein, grandson of the Prophet, in his attempt to oust the usurper Yezid from the position which he occupied as head of the new faith.

After their expulsion from Syria, the tribe migrated eastward into Persia, where they wandered about as pastoral nomads for a great many years, and where they bred and multiplied so greatly as to cause alarm to the Persian monarch. It was during this Persian sojourn that the race gained its undoubted admixture of Persian blood, and where they acquired certain distinct Persian characteristics. Owing to the hostility of the Persian king they were obliged to leave Persia, and according to tradition, they moved under the leadership of one Jalal Khan south-east into Mekran, then an almost uninhabited tract to which no one laid any definite claims. From Mekran they gradually spread all over the tract now called Baluchistan, having in their progress driven into India certain Hindu dynasties and peoples which inhabited certain parts of the country.

The probabilities are therefore, that the Baluchis are a race of Arab stock which, during the progress of its emigration to its present holdings, acquired an admixture of Persian blood, their original speech also being entirely superseded by a dialect of the Persian. It has been maintained by some that the Baluchis are a race of Turkish stock, and certain of their tribal and other customs favour this theory ; but although a certain Turkoman as well as Persian admixture does very probably enter into the Baluch, the probabilities are in favour of their traditional Arab origin.

Of early Baluch history very little is known, and what little there is, is mainly traditional, unsupported by any written historical records of which none exist among the people. Their traditions have it that Jalal Khan, who led them from Persia into Mekran, had four sons, named Rind, Hot, Lashari and Korai, and a daughter, named Jato. There are five distinct tribes which still bear the names of these five children of Jalal Khan. But of them, the descendants of Rind and Lashari soon acquired, by virtue of their superior grit and force of character, a preponderating influence ; so that as the people multiplied and split up into tribes and clans, all these began naturally to come under the influence of, and to group themselves around, either the Rind or the Lashari tribes ; some coming under the political influence and perhaps also the protection of the Rind tribe, while others come in a similar way under the Lashari tribe. In this way all the tribes came to be divided into two great political factions according as their sympathies were with the Rind or with the Lashari. Hence we find that all the Baluch tribes, although they may not belong by descent to either the Rind or Lashari tribes, yet class themselves as being either Rind or Lashari, and this classification constitutes the two broad divisions of the people.

The great traditional hero of the Rind section is one Mir Chakar, who appears to have lived in the 16th century and to have been of great assistance to the Mogul Emperor Humayun, whom he accompanied with a large military following in his reconquest of the Delhi throne. Humayun in gratitude gave Mir Chakar large grants of land on the frontier for the assistance he rendered, and the Baluchi settlements about the southern frontier were in all likelihood founded by Mir Chakar and his followers. Mir Gwahram Khan, the hero of the Lashari section, also played a prominent part in Baluch story, and many are the heroic exploits which tradition has gathered round his name.

It is unnecessary for our purpose to enter into the petty details of Baluch history, or to narrate the political relations which have subsisted between the Khan of Khelat, the ruler of Baluchistan, and the British Indian Government. Those who desire further information on these points will find it in the article "Baluchistan" in the "Encyclopædia Britannica," which contains an excellent description of the country, its people, history, &c.

It is uncertain when the Brahuis, the other and the dominant race in Baluchistan, entered the country, some maintaining that they came before and others that they came in after the Baluchis. The probabilities are that the Brahuis were a tribe of pastoral nomads, either of Dravidian or Iranian stock, who about the 15th or 16th century drove the Baluchis from the hills and valleys abounding in the central province of Khelat, and thus acquired, for a certain period at least, a very real dominance over the Baluch tribes. The ruler of

Baluchistan, known as the Khan of Khelat, is a Brahui, and all the Baluch tribes now acquiesce in regarding the Brahuis as—nominally at least—the dominant race, and the Brahuis enjoy certain privileges not extended to Baluchis. For example, in times of war the Brahui gets wheat flour for his food ration, while the Baluch has to content himself with the coarser joar. For all practical purposes, however, the Brahui dominance has almost become nominal, and is only maintained in so far as they give the ruler to the country. In other respects the several tribes are mutually independent of each other, in times of peace there being little or no cohesion between them, and only a common danger of foreign aggression uniting them for mutual defence.

The Baluchis are Sunni Mahomedans by religion, but they are not a very religious people and are far from being the bigoted fanatics that the Pathans are. The Baluch language, which is a rude dialect of the early Persian, is only colloquial, there being no written language among the people, and as a consequence no such thing as books or literature. Baluchi is spoken throughout the country, except in the province of Khelat, where, owing to its occupation by the dominant Brahuis, Brahui is spoken. Baluchi is divided into two dialects: one the Mekrani or south-western dialect which is spoken in Mekran, Kohistan, and to some extent in Lus; and the Suleimani or north-eastern dialect spoken about our frontier and in Kachh-Gandava, Sarawan and Jhalawan. Scholars are trying to introduce the use of the

Persian character, by using it in recording the traditions, ballads and war songs which are treasured up in the memories of the people, and which have been handed down by memory from generation to generation.

The Baluch tribes are in their political and administrative organization somewhat like a limited monarchy, and in this respect they differ from the Pathan tribes in which the controlling body is the jirga or council of elders. The Baluch tamandar or headman of a tribe (*taman*), has a certain amount of authority ; more at all events than the Khans who are the figure-heads of the various Pathan tribes. Every *taman* or tribe is subdivided into a smaller number of *paras*, at the head of which is a *muquaddam.* Slavery is largely prevalent among them, and polygamy is practised even by the lower orders. Their food consists of wheat, joar and other cereals, and large quantities of pastoral products such as milk, curds and meat. The flesh of the wild ass is regarded as a luxury among them.

Living as they do under very similar conditions of existence, it is not surprising that the Pathan and Baluch present many points of contact in regard to racial characteristics. Manly, frank, brave, strong, inured to hardship and exposure, the Baluch is in many respects a fine type of man. He is not so brutal or so treacherous as the Pathan, and has a higher reputation for truth and fidelity. Free from servility, independent but respectful in bearing, the true Baluch exhibits a strong contempt for the sycophancy which is not uncommon among some races. His wild, free, open-air life, free from the artificial

restraints of civilization, has given him a bold and resolute air of vigour and independence. He is fairly faithful
to his word and knows how to respect fidelity, for there
yet exists among them "a stone or cairn of cursing,
erected as a perpetual memorial of the treachery of one
who betrayed his fellow." He has some chivalry in his
nature, for wild as he is, he will not harm the women
and children even of his bitterest foe. He is not so
bigoted or fanatical as the Pathan, but is like the
Pathan a thief and robber, priding himself in his profi-
ciency at rapine and plunder. He is greatly averse to
manual labour, and is lazy and lacking in industry.
They have a strong predilection for quarreling and
are ready to use their knives on each other on the
slightest provocation. Their national weapons are a
long knife, a sword and a shield. It is noticeable that
the matchlock which is so dear to the heart of the Pathan,
does not enter, except rarely, into his means of offence
and defence. This shews perhaps that the Baluch is ready
to face a foe on equal terms rather than secretly shoot at
him at a distance from behind as is so common among
Pathans. The chief faults of the Baluch are his laziness,
his readiness to quarrel, his dirty personal habits, his
cruel and bloodthirsty nature, and his fondness for
gambling, opium and hemp. "Blood for blood" is his
motto, and though he will hospitably entertain a stranger
seeking his shelter, he would not hesitate to rob and murder
him the moment he left his roof, if by so doing he could
gain any advantage. Nevertheless the Baluch is on the

whole a decidedly fine type of Oriental, and most of those who have had any personal dealings with them, speak highly of them as a race.

The Baluch is an expert in horse and camel breeding, the Baluch breed of these animals enjoying a high reputation all over the frontier, Afghanistan and Persia, for hardihood and endurance.

Mr. Ibbetson, in the Punjab Census Report of 1881, gives the names of 19 principal and 33 minor Baluch tribes, or 52 in all. In the following list the 19 principal tribes are enumerated first :—

Baluch Tribes.

1. Rind.	27. Hajani.
2. Laghari.	28. Shahrani
3. Jatoi.	29. Sanjrani.
4. Gurchani.	30. Laskani.
5. Lashari.	31. Magassi.
6. Khosa.	32. Ahmadani.
7. Korai.	33. Gabol.
8. Tibbi-Lund.	34. Quandrani.
9. Chandia.	35. Kupchani.
10. Gopang.	36. Aliani.
11. Mazari.	37. Kashak.
12. Hot.	38. Khetran.
13. Nutkani.	39. Bugti or Bogti.
14. Gurmani.	40. Bujrani.
15. Kulachi.	41. Badai.
16. Quasrani.	42. Pachar.
17. Jiskani.	43. Tanwari.
18. Drishak.	44. Jafar.
19. Marri.	45. Hijbani.
20. Petafi.	46. Sargani.
21. Gashkori.	47. Shekhani.
22. Mihrani.	48. Shahani.
23. Bozdar.	49. Lund.
24. Mastoi.	50. Mariani.
25. Mashori.	51. Sakhani.
26. Dasti.	52. Mazkani.

Some of these tribes are within our borders, but most of them are without and independent of our authority. The fighting instinct is keen in all these tribes, and they could all, except perhaps the Khetran, supply excellent recruits for our Native regiments if they could only be got to enlist. Their predilections are for a close hand-to-hand fight with swords, the Bozdar tribe being the only one which has shewn any liking for the matchlock of the Pathan. The Marri tribe, against whom a punitive expedition had to be despatched during the Afghan War to keep it out of mischief, is the most important and powerful of all the Baluch tribes. The Khoshas are another powerful and brave Baluch tribe, but they are notorious cattle-lifters, and though possessing a high reputation for courage, are in ill-repute as having a strong bent towards law-breaking and criminality. It is doubtful whether the Khetrans should not be classified as Pathans, but they class themselves as Baluch and are usually regarded as such. They are not very warlike, but are industrious and law-abiding. They are mainly agriculturists and are rich as compared with other Baluch tribes.

It is not necessary to give a descriptive sketch of these tribes as they are scarcely represented at all in our Native army.

CHAPTER III.

PUNJABI MAHOMEDANS.

IN addition to the large and well-defined fighting races inhabiting the Punjab, such as the Sikhs and Pathans, there are a considerable number of smaller fighting castes inhabiting the province, a brief description of them being given below. All these minor fighting clans are ethnologically either of Rajput, Jat, or Tartar descent; but being mostly Mahomedans, they are ever attempting to claim Mogul or Arab origin. These clans are ethnologically not very distinct from some of the less warlike or altogether unwarlike Punjab castes, but having at some period of their history displayed enough grit and strength of character to acquire domination over certain localities, the memory of this supremacy and domination has tended to foster in them that pride of blood and race and that spirit of self-reliance which so largely constitutes the martial instinct. The smaller Mahomedan fighting tribes of the Punjab are often grouped together under the generic term " Punjabi Mahomedan."

Ghakkars.—The Ghakkars, who are now found in the Sub-Himalayan Salt range tracts of the Rawal Pindi, Jhelum and Hazara Districts, are probably a race of Scythian or Tartar origin, the date of their entry into the Punjab being about the 6th century B.C. They are not specially mentioned by the historians of Alexander the Great's Indian invasion, but from a very early period of Indian history they acquired a pre-eminence and pre-dominance over the other inhabitants of the districts in which they lived. In the early periods of their history they were a wild, lawless, tribe of semi-barbarians without any well-defined religious conceptions, and given to polyandry and infanticide, but possessing a high reputa-tion for courage and martial instincts. They first come into prominence during Mahmud of Ghazni's invasion of India, when the Ghakkars are reported to have come with an army of 30,000 men to the help of the Rajput Sovereign Prithwi Raj, in order to defend the country against Mahmud. Though defeated with great slaughter, the Ghakkars gave a very good account of themselves in the battle ; so much so, that Mahmud thought it advisable to leave them severely alone. Early in the 13th century they rebelled against Shahab-ud-din Ghori, but were defeated and compelled to adopt Mahomedanism. They shortly after murdered Shahab-ud-din. Later on, the Emperor Babar attacked and defeated the Ghakkars and captured their capital Pharwala, but respecting their courage the Emperor gave them extensive grants of land as military fiefs to be held by them in return for loyal support and military aid to the Delhi throne. From this time to the ultimate downfall of the Mogul Empire they remained true to the Delhi throne, and then passed under Sikh rule, but not without first making a fierce struggle for liberty. On the annexation of the Punjab they passed under our rule, but discontent was smouldering in their midst, and four years after annexation they attempted to rebel. During the Mutiny also they gave some trouble, but were kept well in hand by the able body of men who fortunately were at the head of affairs in the Punjab in those troublesome times.

According to the last Census they numbered only some 29,000 souls, mostly in the hills in the districts of Rawal Pindi, Hazara and Jhelum.

Ghakkars make excellent soldiers. They are an exceptionally fine race, proud, brave, high-spirited and self-respecting. They are regarded in the localities they occupy as *Sahu* or gentlemen. Their leading men display a high-bred courtesy and are very gentlemanly in their features and deportment. They have five clans among themselves, *viz.*, the Bugial, Iskandeal, Firozal, Admal, and Surangal.

Awans.—The Awans, who now number about 609,000 souls, are freely distributed along the Salt Range tracts, being found most largely in the Jhelum, Rawal Pindi, Hazara and Peshawar Districts ; and also, but not to so large an extent, in the districts of Kohat, Bannu, Dera Ismail Khan, Shahpur, Gujrat, Jullunder and Sialkot. They are probably a race of Scythian origin, who at some remote period entered India through some of the Derajat passes and then fought their way northwards. It is probable that at one period of their history they were the dominant race over a considerable area along the Salt Range. According to their traditions they were converted to Mahomedanism under the slave kings of Delhi, Kutub-ud-din the great slave king being largely instrumental in their conversion. Shortly after his death however, before the tribe had quite settled down into their new faith, they appear to have reverted to Hinduism, and were then again re-converted to Islam. Owing to this vacillating conversion, the Awans retain to this day certain Hindu tendencies in their midst, Hindu names occurring not unfrequently among them, and some going to the length of employing Brahmins as their household priests.

They are strong and hardy men and make good soldiers, but are quarrelsome and vindictive to a degree. They possess, to a certain extent, a Pathan-like proclivity for blood-letting, but on the whole are a well-behaved and law-abiding race, possessing much courage, spirit, and self-respect.

Sials.—The Sials, who occupy considerable tracts in the Punjab District of Jhang, are a tribe or caste of Rajput Mahomedans who, during the 18th century, played a considerable part in the history of that locality. Their traditions have it that about the 13th century their Chief named Rai Shankar, held considerable sway in the western parts of the North-West Provinces, but that on the confusion and disorder consequent on the Mahomedan invasions of India, they took advantage of the lack of organised and ordered government to move westward into the Punjab, where, under the leadership of Sial, the son of Rajah Rai Shankar, they conquered a considerable tract of country for themselves from Shahpur to Mooltan. They were converted to Islam in the 14th century, but traces of their early Hindu faith are still found among them. On the downfall of the Mogul Empire they became a practically independent tribe and continued such till finally overthrown by the Sikhs.

The Sials number about 100,000, and are a fine race, brave, self-respecting and hardy. The memory of their dominant position for nearly a century has given them considerable pride of race, which enhances their fighting value. They are physically big and strong men, rather rude and rough in their demeanour. They are pastoral by instinct, though they also engage in some agriculture. During the Mutiny the Sial Chief remained loyal, and rendered active assistance by raising a small body of cavalry from his tribe for Imperial use.

Gujars.—The Gujars are ethnologically a race of Tartar or Scythian stock, and now number over 700,000, distributed freely over the centre, north and west of the Punjab. They are found in large numbers in the districts of Umballa, Hoshiarpore, Gurudaspore, Gujrat and Hazara ; and also, but not so largely, in the districts of Hissar, Gurgaon, Delhi, Karnal, Jullunder, Ludhiana and Ferozepore. Early in the Christian era, and for about a century before, the Gujars played a very important part in the history of northern India, and they were, for some time, the dominant people about the Peshawar border and a little south-east of it. They even fought their way as far south as Rajputana, and established a small kingdom there. Khanishka the great Buddhist king appears to have belonged to this tribe, and they spread not only southward, but northwards into Jammu, where a Gujar chief held sway for a long period. Their wide distribution over the Punjab is accounted for by their once extensive domination.

The Gujar is not now thought very highly of as a soldier, and doubtless he has degenerated much since the time when he was one of the dominant factors in the Punjab. Nevertheless, he is physically a well-built and hardy man, and still retains some of his old martial instincts. He has a predilection for cattle-lifting, and is idle and lazy to a degree, so that they are a comparatively poor tribe. He has not the pride and self-respect of the Ghakkar, but is quite as good as some of the castes now enlisted. His character however, varies to some extent, according to the locality from which he comes. Those further east do not hold a high reputation, but those in the western parts of the province, in Rawal Pindi, Hazara, Jhelum and Hoshiarpore, are held in much respect for sober industry and manliness. If properly selected there can be no doubt but that some good recruits could be got from the tribe, which being a comparatively large one, gives a wide field for choice. They are mainly pastoral, but engage also in agriculture to some extent.

Tiwanas.—The Tiwanas are ethnologically closely related to the Sials, and appear like the Sials to be a tribe of Rajput origin which moved from somewhere about the Jamna and Ganges Doab into the Punjab about the 13th or 14th century. They are now mainly found in the

Shahpore District about the Salt range, and are not a very large caste, but have played some part in local history. They are a partly pastoral and partly agricultural tribe, and make capital soldiers.

Gondals.—This tribe occupies portions of territory in the Shahpore and Gujrat Districts between the Jhelum and Chenab and are supposed to have been originally Chauhan Rajputs who were converted to Islam about the 14th century. They are mainly pastoral and have an evil reputation for cattle-stealing, but they are physically a fine race and make good fighting material.

Chibbs.—The Chibbs are a small clan of Rajput Mahomedans who were converted to Islam about the 17th century. They occupy parts of the Jammu Hills and of the district of Gujrat. They make good soldiers, being of good physique, and possessing much pride of blood and race. Their numerical paucity makes recruiting among them to any extent impossible. Their social standing among other castes is high.

Sattis.—The Sattis are also a caste of Rajput origin, but are now Mahomedan by religion. They occupy the hills in the Hazara and Rawal Pindi Districts. Their numbers are not large. They are of fairly good physique and possess much pride of race, but their martial qualities have not been quite established; some officers speaking disparagingly of them, while others hold them in high repute as soldiers. Carefully selected they could doubtless give a few good recruits to the Native army, but they are too small to merit much attention.

Janjuas.—The Janjuas are another clan of Salt Range Rajputs who have been converted to Mahomedanism. At one period of their history they held sway over a considerable portion of the Salt Range, but were driven eastward by the Ghakkars and Awans. In character they are very much like these two tribes, and like them they make good soldiers. They are not very numerous.

Dogars.—If there are any representatives of this caste in our Native army, the number must be very small. Considering however, that at one period the Dogars offered a very stout resistance to Sikh domination, and that even now they have a rather unenviable reputation for turbulence, there is probably still some fight in them. Perhaps they have not been exploited sufficiently, and their characteristics are not very well known. They should not be confounded with the Dogras who are quite a distinct race. They claim to be Chauhan Rajputs, who were converted to Mahomedanism. They number in all about 55,000, and are found mostly in the district of Ferozepore, and also in those of Lahore, Hissar, Hoshiarpore, Amritsar, Sialkot, Gurudaspore and Jullunder. They are physically a good-looking race, of good physique, and are not wanting in courage, though, as has been said, they have not been tested sufficiently.

Kharrals.—The Kharrals, who number in all about 60,000, are ethnologically Jats or Rajputs, but Mahomedans by religion. They are found mostly in the Montgomery District where they number 22,000. They are also found in the Lahore and Gurgaon Districts, but in smaller numbers; and scattered settlements of them exist in Sirsa, Jhang, Mooltan, and Bhawalpore Districts. The triangular tract of country which has the Chenab and Ravi for its two sides, and its base the boundary line of the Hafizabad, Sharakpur and Chunian tahsils, is inhabited by certain castes and tribes which are classified in two great divisions, known as the "Little Ravi Tribes" and the "Great Ravi Tribes." The former are mainly agricultural, the latter mainly pastoral. Of the Great Ravi tribes, the Kharrals are the most important. The Kharrals are themselves divided into two great branches, the Upper Ravi Kharrals and the Lower Ravi Kharrals, the latter being also known as the Kamalia Kharrals.

The Kharrals are a hardy, well-built, and good-looking tribe, possessing the martial instinct to a high degree, and make very good soldiers. They are, however, lawless and turbulent, much given to cattle-stealing, and are extremely lazy and lacking in thrift and industry. They gave a lot of trouble during the Mutiny, and succeeded in committing some raids on Hindu villages where there was any hope of their getting a substantial booty. They should not be confounded with the Karrals.

Ahirs.—The Ahirs are a pastoral tribe, who, in the Punjab, number about 125,000. They live mostly by rearing and breeding cattle, and are found in the Punjab, mostly in the district of Gurgaon, where they number 71,000, and also in Hissar, Rohtak and Delhi Districts. They are a hardworking and industrious tribe, with no great reputation for soldierly instincts, but they are strong and

hardy men, and could supply some good recruits. They
are partly Hindu and partly Mahomedan by religion.
(See also Ch. xiii.)

Khokars.—The Khokars are a large and widely distributed caste of Mahomedan Rajputs, numbering about
150,000 souls. They are found mostly in the Lahore,
Shahpur, Bhawalpore and Jhang Districts, but are also
found further west, where, owing to the supremacy of
Islam, they call themselves Jats, and have concocted a
purely mythical tradition that they are descended from
Kutub-Shah of Ghazni. They are of undoubted Hindu
origin, and at one time were the dominant race in Jhang.
They are a law-abiding and industrious tribe, of good
physique, and make excellent soldiers when carefully
selected.

Bhattis.—The Bhattis are a large and widely distributed tribe, numbering about 350,000 in the Punjab, and
found there mostly in the districts of Amritsar, Gurudaspore, Sialkot, Lahore, Gujranwala, Ferozepore, Multan,
Jhang and Montgomery, The Bhattis are one of the most
important of the Rajput tribes, and have played a conspicuous part in Punjab history. They are still the dominant people in the Rajput State of Jaisalmere, and form
also a prominent and important factor in the State of
Bikaneer. The Bhattis of the Punjab are a very fine
race, tall and muscular, with refined features and well-bred
ways. Possessed of much of their old soldierly instincts,
and proud of their history and themselves, they make
capital soldiers.

Traditionally the Bhattis are Lunar, Jadubansi, Rajputs, descended from Krishna, the Hindu deity. It is probable that at one period of Indian history their sway extended along the whole of the Salt Range, but that they were driven from the Salt Range further north into Kashmir by Scythian or Tartar invaders, and also southwards into the tracts below the Sutlej. Towards the south of the province the tribe has given its name to the tract known as Bhattiana, lying about Sirsa and Hissar.

They are both agricultural and pastoral by occupation. In the Punjab they are largely Mahomedans by religion.

Karrals.—The Karrals, who should not be confounded with the Kharrals, are a small caste of Rajputs who have only been recently converted to Mahomedanism. Their holdings are mainly in the Salt Range tracts in the Hazara District where they number about 12,000 only. They make very good cultivators, being industrious and hard-working. They have no great reputation among their neighbours for martial instincts, but this is perhaps due to their law-abiding nature, the mistake being very prevalent among Indian tribes that lawlessness and turbulence are the only tests for courage. Some Karrals are to be found in the ranks of the Native army, and they make very fair soldiers. Like most of the Mahomedan tribes of the Punjab, they are ever attempting to claim relationship with either the Arabs or Moguls, the Karrals claiming for themselves a Mogul origin; but there are absolutely no grounds for this claim.

Julahas.—The Julahas are weavers by profession, and are ethnologically probably of aboriginal descent ; but have, in the course of centuries of contact with superior races, acquired an admixture of better blood. They are mainly Mahomedans, and have got, even among their co-religionists, an evil reputation for bumptiousness. They have given a great deal of trouble from time to time by their criminality and turbulence, but their soldierly instincts are decidedly poor, and they are only mentioned here because a good many of them manage to smuggle themselves into our Native army by calling themselves by some other more desirable name. Their social standing is very low, being only a step removed from the Chamars, and they should not be enlisted.

CHAPTER IV.

Sikhs.

During the 14th and 15th centuries of the Christian era, the whole of India, and more especially the Punjab, was in a state of profound ferment both political and religious. The entrance into the country in large numbers of the Moguls and other Central Asian peoples, full of energy, vigour and warlike instincts, as well as zealous propagandists of their Mahomedan faith, had tended to arouse the Indian mind from its centuries of lethargy, and had infused a new spirit of enquiry and spiritual unrest among the people. Sikhism, the religion founded by Baba Nanak, the first Sikh guru, really had its indirect origin in the spiritual unrest and enquiry which resulted from the dominance of an energetic and intelligent Mahomedan race ; and though in after years the Sikhs and Mahomedans were sworn and implacable foes, there can be no doubt but that the early religious impressions of Nanak were largely the result of the Mogul conquest and its attendant consequences.

Nanak the founder of Sikhism, was born in the year 1469 A.D., and died in the year 1538, though the date of his death is sometimes given as 1539 A.D. He was thus contemporary with Babar and Humayon, the first two Mogul Emperors. His place of birth was a small village named Talwandi in the Sharakpore tahsil of the Lahore District, his father belonging to the Bedi sub-caste of the great Punjabi Khattri caste. His father appears to have been like all Khattris a small merchant or tradesman, and to have occupied a position of some influence in his native village. According to Sikh tradition, Nanak from a very early age exhibited a strong religious bent of mind, and at a period of life when it would have been only natural to think mostly of pleasure and enjoyment, he appears to have given himself up almost wholly to brooding and meditation. On attaining manhood he became a regular jogi or religious mendicant, and in this capacity, as is wont among the fraternity, he seems to have wandered all over India from one religious shrine to another, and even to have found his way through Afghanistan and Persia into Arabia. However this may be, he certainly came largely into contact with the best Mahomedanism, and the tradition is still extant that at an early age he received religious instruction from a Mahomedan fakir.

During his lifetime, he does not seem to have made many converts or to have had any extensive religious following. But with that keen eye to detect ability when it exists in others which able men invariably possess, Nanak attached to himself a following, which, though numerically small, was composed of men of sterling quality. The religious doctrines taught by him were a very rational mixture of what was best in Hinduism and Mahomedanism. Thus, he taught the unity and goodness of God, as opposed to the prevailing Hindu doctrine of a bewildering multiplicity of

deities both good and bad, but mostly the latter. Keenly
alive to the evils and degradation of the caste system, he
taught the spiritual and religious equality of all men,
though he had no absurd socialistic notions in his head.
He rejected the pretentions of the Brahmins and refused
to grant them the almost divine honours they claimed
from the ignorant. What will appear still more surprising
when one remembers the bitter feud that afterwards
came to exist between the Sikhs and Mahomedans, is
that Nanak taught that Hindu and Mahomedan were
alike in the eyes of God, and should live in peace and
harmony with one another. In short, the religion taught
by Nanak was a refined Hinduism purged of its grossness
by the more elevated religious precepts of Islam. Sikhism,
as taught by Nanak and his successors, bears to Hinduism
much the same relation that Protestantism does to
Roman Catholicism, being nothing more than an attempt
to free popular Hinduism of its errors and grossness.
Nanak was a religious teacher pure and simple ; he did
not meddle with politics, and he never attempted to found
anything more than a religious order.

Nanak had two sons, Lachmi Das and Sri Chand by
name. The latter was, like his father, of a strongly
religious bent, and lived and died an ascetic. He in his
turn founded a sect of Sikhism known as the Udasi sect.
This sect may be described as that of Sikh Puritanism,
and is much given to austerities and religious fervour.
Lachmi, or Lakhmi Das, the elder brother of Sri Chand,
does not appear to have been remarkable for anything in

particular, and his death caused no gap to be felt in the ranks of Sikhism.

Nanak set aside both his sons, as he did not think them of sufficient merit to succeed him, and chose as his successor in the guruship one of his disciples, Lehna by name, who was like Nanak a Khattri by caste, but of the Tihun subdivision of the caste. Nanak conferred on Lehna the name of Angad (angad=own body), on account of Lehna's signal devotion to his commands and person, and Lehna is therefore usually known as Guru Angad. He continued in the guruship till his death in 1552 A.D. The fourteen years of his administration were not remarkable for anything in particular, nor did the new faith make much progress under him; but he loyally carried out the pacific and liberal religious policy of Nanak, and kept alive that feeling of religious fervour and integrity which Nanak had infused into his few followers.

Angad chose as his successor one of his followers named Amardas, having like Nanak, with a wise liberality and discretion, set aside his own sons for one better fitted for the post. Amardas was guru for 22 years from 1552 to 1574, and was also a Khattri by caste, but of the Bhalla sub-caste. During his tenure of office, the Sikh sect of Narainjanis came into existence, but he excommunicated the bigoted Udasi sect.

Amardas was succeeded by Guru Ramdas, a Sodhi Khattri by birth, who held office from 1574 to 1581. Guru Ramdas's seven years' tenure of office is remarkable in that he succeeded in organising and consolidating the new faith, which, though still small and insignificant numerically, was beginning to attract attention. Ramdas also built the Harmandal or golden temple of Amritsar, and virtually founded Amritsar itself, thus giving to Sikhism a great centralised abode of worship which all Sikhs could regard and look up to as the Mecca and Medina of their faith. Under his successor Guru Arjan, who was guru from 1581 to 1606, Sikhism made rapid progress. Arjan, a man of strong practical ability and common sense, was by nature anything but a brooding and meditative recluse unconcerned with the ordinary affairs of life. He compiled from the teachings and writings of Nanak and his successors, the Granth or sacred book of the Sikhs, but this must not be confounded with the Granth written by Nanak, and which is popularly known as the Adi Granth or original Granth. He also carried out extensive commercial transactions and thus enriched the community. He further gave them a properly organised system for the government of the community, and in place of voluntary and spasmodic, though often liberal, pecuniary contributions to the communal purse, he instituted a regular but not excessive system of taxation, which brought in a regular and fixed income for communal purposes. Arjan was an ambitious man, anxious to play a prominent part, as indeed his abilities well fitted him to do ; and he was thus gradually led into taking a part in public and political affairs. It was during his guruship that the Sikhs first appear in history as a rising political factor.

The first important act in the political history of the Sikhs was the aid they rendered the rebel Mogul Prince Khushru in his rebellion against the Delhi throne. After the rebellion was crushed, Arjan was summoned by the Emperor to Delhi, and was there imprisoned till his death in 1606. The tradition among the Sikhs however, is that he mysteriously disappeared while bathing in the Ravi. During his imprisonment he appears to have been subjected to much persecution and indignity, and thus were sown the first seeds of that bitter and implacable enmity which afterwards came to exist between Mahomedan and Sikh.

Guru Arjan, a Sodhi Khattri by caste, was succeeded by his son Har Govind, and from this time till the last guru, all belonged to the Sodhi sub-caste of the Khattri caste. These gurus are, therefore, collectively known as the Sodhis. Har Govind was guru from 1606 to 1638. With the memory of the cruelties and indignities suffered by his father fresh in his memory, it is not to be wondered at that Har Govind turned aside from the peaceful religious life of Nanak and the earlier gurus, and burned with a desire to avenge his father's fate. He does not appear to have been a man with a strong religious bent, but to have been a practical and adventuresome man of the world, with an innate love of war. He therefore urged the necessity for knowing the use of arms among his followers and strove to fire them with his own warlike instincts. He not only permitted but encouraged the use of flesh—except that of cows and of unclean animals—as articles of diet, as tending to improve the strength and physique of the race, and he did his utmost to instil manliness, self-reliance, and courage among his followers. Actuated by such motives and principles, he soon got mixed up in the rebellions which the royal sons of the Delhi throne were ever raising against their fathers, in which the Sikhs aided first one side and then another according as their interests dictated.

Guru Har Govind was succeeded by his grandson Har Rai, his son Garditta—reverenced up to this day as one of the most saintly of the Sikhs—having died in early manhood. Har Rai was guru from 1638 to 1660. He too mixed himself up for a time in the political intrigues of the Mogul Court, but settled down ultimately to a quiet life. Har Rai's successor was his younger son Har Kissen (1660—64), the elder son Ram Rai having been set aside by his father as unworthy to hold the guruship. Both Har Rai and Har Kissen continued the policy originated by Arjan and developed by Har Govind, of taking part in the political intrigues of the Delhi Court, and thus they not only brought the Sikhs prominently to notice, but frequently got them into serious trouble with the Delhi Emperors, who very naturally retaliated on the Sikhs—often in a most brutal manner—for the aid they rendered rebellious sons, relatives, and governors. The Sikhs also about this time began to make themselves a further source of trouble and anxiety to the Delhi Emperors, because of the extensive plundering expeditions they began to be constantly engaged in ; and, it must in justice be admitted, that the Sikhs were the first aggressors in the bitter feud which afterwards existed between the two races.

The ninth guru was Teg Bahadur, the third son of Har Govind, and the grand uncle of Har Kissen. Teg Bahadur, a gloomy, morose and austere man inclined to bigotry and fanaticism, accentuated to a marked degree the prevailing tendency among the Sikhs to assist rebel princes and governors against the ruling dynasty, and to plunder and raid whenever the opportunity occurred. The Sikhs therefore in the days of Aurangzebe came naturally and rightly to be regarded as a dangerous sect of freebooters, the extermination of whom would prove a public blessing. Teg Bahadur carried out this policy of plunder and rebellion to a far greater extent than any of his predecessors, and being naturally of a fiery and resolute nature, soon made himself particularly obnoxious to Aurangzebe, then Emperor. Teg Bahadur who was guru from 1664 to 1675, was ultimately captured by the Moguls and put to a shameful and cruel death, a large number of his followers sharing the same fate.

During all this period from the days of Arjan to Teg Bahadur, the Sikhs were steadily increasing in numbers, because the absence of caste among them and the social and religious equality inculcated by Sikhism, naturally drew to its fold a large number of converts from the lower castes, who were only too glad to improve their social and religious status. A large number of

Churas or sweepers thus entered the fold of Sikhism ; but at the same time a good many of the higher Jats, Khattris, and to some extent Rajputs also, embraced Sikhism for its inherent merits ; being drawn thereto by the zeal and eloquence of the gurus, who were all of them in their own way, men of ability and merit. Indeed, but for the great discretion shewn in the choice of the several gurus, it is very doubtful whether Sikhism would ever have attained to any prominence ; for, as has already been stated, Nanak did not attempt to do anything more than to spread a quiet, inoffensive, tolerant and a purer Hinduism than was ordinarily prevalent.

The tenth and last, and the greatest of all the gurus was Govind Singh (1675—1708), the son of Teg Bahadur. Under Govind Singh the Sikhs were finally converted from a semi-religious sect into a strong political community, full of warlike ardour. Born at Patna while his father was there on a pilgrimage, Govind Singh long brooded in silence over the cruelties suffered by his father and his fellow Sikhs. On attaining manhood his one idea was to revenge himself on the Mahomedan rulers of the land, whose barbarities were perpetuated all over the unhappy country they ruled, or rather misruled. A man of great ability, of practical and resolute character, with a keen and innate liking for war, rendered more formidable by a deep religious bias, Govind Singh was by nature well fitted to be a leader of men. Before venturing to carry out his projects of revenge against, and liberty from, the Mahomedan yoke,

he had the wisdom to consolidate his followers and revive
their flagging spirits, as owing to Aurangzebe's brutal
persecutions, all organisation among the Sikhs had almost
ceased to exist.   During several years of retirement he
quietly consolidated his followers. To nerve them for
the stern work he had in store for them, he preached
that war, especially against the Mahomedans, was the
first duty of the Sikh ; and to give force to his preach-
ing he instituted certain customs which would keep
the thought of war constantly in their minds.   He conferred on all those Sikhs who should follow his precepts
faithfully the title of *Khalsa* or the pure or elect ; and
in order to enter the ranks of the Khalsa, he instituted—
or rather re-instituted with some modifications—an initia-
tory religious rite called the *pahul* (literally means gate or
way of entrance).   This rite consisted in drinking in the
presence of at least five of the faithful, a mixture of sugar
and water, stirred by a two-edged dagger, the noviciate
taking at the same time certain vows of constancy and
courage.   The members of the Khalsa were to be called
Singhs or lions, to denote that their mission in life was the
exercise of warlike courage, and to distinguish them from
those Sikhs who refused to follow his teachings, and who
preferred to be mainly a religious sect.   He also instituted
the five Kakas to distinguish the Khalsa from the other
Sikh sects, and emphasise the warlike mission of the
Khalsa.   He tried to unite high and low by altogether
abolishing caste distinctions ; for, though Nanak had done
his best to discourage caste distinctions and prejudices,

they had still lingered on in the Sikh community. Govind Singh wished to abolish every vestige of caste, and to admit all who took the *pahul* and entered the Khalsa into terms of absolute equality and privilege, the only distinction to be observed being the natural superiorities and inferiorities which exist among men in regard to character and ability. This gave great offence to some of the Sikhs recruited from the higher castes, but Govind Singh was largely joined by men of castes like the Jat and Khattri, possessed of much sterling manliness of character.

Having done all in his power to rouse the dormant warlike instincts of his followers, Govind Singh emerged from his retirement and, at the age of about 30, began his career of war and revenge. It is unnecessary for our purpose to enter into the many details of his chequered career. Suffice it to say that he was defeated over and over again, and his relatives and followers were put to most brutal and revolting deaths. But that indomitable and resolute spirit which he had done his best to instil into his followers, allowed no defeat to crush or cow him, and he succeeded in doing an immense amount of harm to the Delhi throne. Finally, after many years of constant conflict, Aurangzebe found it to his advantage to come to terms with him, and Govind Singh, worn out with age and the constant and wearying anxieties of war, consented to live in peace with the Emperor and to accept from him a high command in Hyderabad. He was murdered by a Pathan while holding this command, at Naderh or Nandair on the Godavery,

and to this day there is a colony of Sikhs around those
parts, known as the Nandair Sikhs. Nandair or Naderh
is called by the Sikhs Abchalnagar (or place of departure),
and many of the faithful Khalsa still make pilgrimages
to the place in honour of their great guru.

The life and teaching of Govind Singh thus resulted in the Sikhs being broken up into two great divisions,
viz., the Khalsa Sikhs or Singhs, a political community of
warriors; and the non-Khalsa Sikhs who are not Singhs,
but who are a purely religious and non-political sect of
Hindus. These latter again, as will be seen later, are
subdivided into numerous sects.

Govind Singh had declared shortly before his death
that no one should succeed him in the guruship, and that
the office of guru should reside in the community as
a whole. After his death therefore, though the abler men
among the Sikhs naturally came to the front as leaders,
they were never called gurus. The most famous of these
was Banda, a man somewhat after the pattern of Teg
Bahadur, stern, grave and morose, but resolute and brave.

After Govind Singh's death, the enmity between Mahomedan and Sikh waxed more fierce, and the succeeding
years were but one record of constant but spasmodic
fighting between the two races, in which victory and
defeat were evenly divided between them, both parties
displaying an implacable enmity and a brutal spirit
of revenge which spared neither age nor sex. Every
advantage which the Delhi Emperors gained over the
Sikhs was invariably followed by terrible and brutal

retribution, men, women and children being put to most
painful and revolting deaths ; and it must be admitted that
the Sikhs themselves were not slow to retaliate whenever
the fortune of war was on their side. At one time the
Mogul persecution of the Sikhs was so great as practically
to destroy all cohesion and organisation among them, and
for a short time the Sikhs almost ceased to exist as a
corporate community. But as the Mogul Empire became
gradually weaker and weaker, breaking up through its
own inherent rottenness as well as by the attacks of its
enemies, the Sikhs began to reconsolidate, and to nerve
themselves for the fight for independence. The absence
of all order and government in those dark years during
which the Mogul Empire was hastening to its fall, was
eminently favourable to the schemes of bold and rest-
less spirits who, combining ability and ambition with
courage, were naturally led to attempt great things for
themselves. As a consequence of the times, we find a
great many brave and able men collecting a following
round them, and attempting to carve out kingdoms
for themselves from the ruin of the Mogul Empire ;
and so also, it came to pass that the bolder spirits
among the Sikhs thrust themselves forward as leaders,
and collecting round them a following, soon began
to attempt not only independence but empire. Thus
in course of time the Sikhs came to group themselves
around several distinct Chiefs, who formed and organised
the Sikhs into confederacies known as *misls*, and till the
advent to power of Ranjit Singh these *misls* continued

to exist, and to exercise within themselves the functions of government. For some time before and at the date of Ranjit Singh's birth there were twelve misls known as under—

Ahluwalia misl.	Phulkian misl.
Bhangi misl.	Singpuria misl.
Kanhiya misl.	Karora Singhia misl.
Ramgharia misl.	Nishania misl.
Sukarchakia misl.	Dulelwalia misl.
Nakaiya misl.	Shahid misl.

These misls were constantly at war with the other Mahomedan and Hindu Chiefs around them, and in 1761 they united with the Mahrattas to oppose Ahmad Shah Abdalli, and though they received a crushing defeat, they exhibited much courage. They were also constantly at war with each other till the rise of Ranjit Singh, who belonged to the Sukarchakia misl, and who, having defeated and subdued all the other misls, united all the Sikhs under him as their king.

It is unnecessary for our purpose to say more about the rise of Ranjit Singh than to remark that he gradually raised the Sikhs into a position of political dominance, and that he overran the whole of the Punjab.

Born therefore, as a peaceable and tolerant religion, Sikhism was gradually transformed from a purely religious movement by the persecutions of fanatical bigots like Aurangzebe and the inhuman brutalities of his weak and debauched successors into a military and political movement directed against the weakness and inhumanity of the later Mogul Emperors.

The national character of the Sikhs has been determined mainly by four causes, *viz.*, his ethnological origin, by the early persecutions under which Sikhism was nurtured, by his hatred of the Mussulman, and by the knowledge of his once dominant position. The better classes of Sikhs are mainly drawn from certain Punjab tribes like the Jat and Khattri, which as far back as we have any historical evidence, have always shewn a certain amount of sturdy grit and manly independence of character. The finest specimen of the Sikh, namely, the Jat Sikh, possesses all the virtues of the Jat of the Punjab, added to which are the many virtues developed by Sikhism itself. Speaking of the Jat of the Sikh tracts, Mr. lbbetson says :—" His manners do not bear the impress of generations of wild freedom which marks the races of our frontier mountains. But he is more honest, more industrious, more sturdy and no less manly than they. Sturdy independence indeed, and patient vigorous labour are his strongest characteristics. The Jat is of all Punjab races the most impatient of tribal or communal control, and the ones which assert the freedom of the individual most strongly. As a rule, a Jat is a man who does what seems right in his own eyes, and sometimes what seems wrong also, and will not be said nay by any man. I do not mean, however, that he is turbulent. As a rule, he is far from being so. He is independent, and he is self-willed ; but he is reasonable, peaceably inclined if left alone, and not difficult to manage. He is usually content to cultivate his fields and pay his revenue in peace and quietness if people will let him do so; though, when he does go wrong, he takes to anything from gambling to murder, with perhaps a preference for stealing other people's wives and cattle."

In the Sikh these characteristics of the Jat are blended together with certain other traits which are the result of his recent political supremacy. He is self-respecting to a degree, and regards and looks upon himself and his race with just pride. The essentially tolerant spirit of Sikhism as taught by Nanak has removed from the Sikhs the religious prejudices of the Hindu on the one hand, and the rancour and fanaticism of the Mahomedan on the other. He is far less blinded by religious intolerance than either, and in most things is a level-headed, sober-minded man with keen practical instincts.

As a soldier the Sikh displays a cool, quiet, and resolute courage, and he is much less likely to lose his head in the excitement of battle than the Pathan. He has even in the ordinary affairs of life his passions well under control, so that, being accustomed to habits of self-restraint, he knows how to keep cool and unexcited in moments of difficulty and danger. He is therefore, much less liable to sudden panic than the Pathan, though perhaps he has not that dash and élan which characterises the Pathan in his highest warlike mood.

The higher classes of Sikhs display a high-bred courtesy which is very pleasing, and their deportment is marked by much grace. Even the poorer classes—especially among our sepoys—carry themselves with much quiet

but manly elegance, and their splendid physique adds
to the dignity of their bearing.

Taken as a whole, the Sikh is one of the finest types
of man to be found in Asia. He is independent without
being insolent, resolute and firm in character, remarkably
free from the petty bias and prejudices which run ram-
pant in a land of prejudices like India ; respects himself,
and as a consequence, commands the respect of others ; is
a soldier by instinct and tradition ; regards cowardice as
worse than crime ; and with his splendid physique and well-
bred ways is altogether one of the finest Oriental races.

The tracts occupied by the Sikhs are divided into two
great divisions by the river Sutlej. The tracts lying to
the west of the Sutlej or the trans-Sutlej Sikh tracts are
popularly known as Manjha, and the Sikhs occupying
these tracts are commonly known as Manjha or Manjhi
Sikhs. The Cis-Sutlej tracts lying east of the Sutlej are
known as Malwa, and the Sikhs of these tracts are known
as Malwa or Malwai Sikhs.

Sikhs may be classified in three ways, *viz.*—

      (1) Ethnologically, *i.e.*, by the tribe, race or caste
          to which they belong ;

      (2) According to the religious sect of Sikhism
          to which they belong ; and

      (3) According to their political convictions as
          Khalsa or non-Khalsa Sikhs.

We shall first give a brief description of the several castes
which have given converts in any numbers to Sikhism,
and then a description of the religious sects of the Sikhs.

Garu Nanak, although he did not absolutely prohibit caste, did all he could to discourage it. This policy of passive discouragement of caste, rather than of active and pronounced hostility to it, continued till the days of the last guru, Govind Singh, who unhesitatingly condemned caste and strove to admit all castes on equal terms into the fold of the Khalsa. Owing to this policy, first of discouragement and then of open condemnation of caste, it has come about that all castes can freely enter Sikhism ; and although practically Sikhs of the lower castes are not admitted into terms of social equality with those of the higher castes, still in theory the equality does exist. In Sikhism therefore, men of all castes are to be found, and it must not be supposed, as is very often the case, that Sikhism represents an. ethnological expression, or that the Sikhs are a race ethnologically distinct from the other Punjab races. The principal castes which have given converts to Sikhism are the Punjabi Jats, Khattris, Chuhras, Kambohs, Kalals, Labanas, Tarkhans, Chamars and Julahas, and to a minor degree Rajputs and Brahmins. As caste has to a certain extent an ethnological basis, and represents a difference of racial origin, it follows that the Sikhs are ethnologically composed of several distinct but allied races, welded together into one by a common bond of religion and polity.

We now proceed to describe some of the salient features and characteristics of the principal castes and tribes which have given converts in any considerable numbers to Sikhism.

Jat Sikhs.—The Jat has been dealt with in a separate chapter and a description of the Jat Sikh will be found lower on. The principal Jat sub-castes inhabiting the Manjha and Malwa are twenty-one in number, the total population being in all about one and a quarter million. These twenty-one sub-castes are the Dhillon, Virk, Sindhu, Bhular, Man, Her, Buttar, Odi, Bal, Pannun, Mahal, Aulak, Gil, Sidhu, Barar, Dhariwal, Sara, Mangat, Dhindsa, Gandhi and Chahil. Of these, the Sindhu, Gil and Sidhu are the largest in number, the next in numerical importance being the Dhillon, Virk, Man, Barar and Dhariwal. All these sub-castes supply excellent fighting material, and though they are not Sikh in the bulk, a very considerable portion are.

Khattri Sikhs.—The Khattris are a Punjab caste of merchants and traders. They claim to be descended from the ancient Kshatriyas of the early Hindu epics, but this is doubtful. Although traders by profession, they are far from being anything like the buniya, for the Punjabi Khattri is a fine, steady, manly fellow, with much spirit and courage in him. All the Sikh gurus were Khattris by birth, so that Sikh Khattris are held in high estimation among the Sikhs. All Khattris are not, however, Sikh by religion, a considerable number being Hindus. They number about half a million, and are found in the largest numbers in the Ludhiana, Amritsar, Sialkot, Gujranwala and Rawal Pindi Districts, and considerable numbers are also found in the Umballa, Hoshiarpore, Lahore and Jhang Districts.

Kamboh Sikhs.—The Kambohs, who number about 150,000, are found mostly in the districts of Karnal, Umballa, Jullunder, Montgomery, Lahore and Amritsar. They are agriculturists by profession, and have a very high reputation as such. About twenty-three per cent. of them are Sikhs by religion, thirty-seven per cent. are Mahomedans, and forty per cent. are Hindus. Kamboh Sikhs are very numerous in Kapurthala, and they make very good soldiers, being of fine physique, and plucky, though they have a reputation for deceit. But they are hardly worse in this respect than many other castes.

Lobana or Labana Sikhs.—The Labana is a Punjab caste, equal to the Jat in social standing. They are carriers by profession, and convey merchandise by bullock and camel transport all over the Punjab. Since the introduction of railways however, their caste profession is steadily declining in value as a means of support, so that large numbers are now obliged to take to agriculture. Owing to their active, open-air life they are generally men of good physique and great powers of endurance. About thirty per cent. are Sikhs by religion, and the Labana Sikh makes a capital soldier, but he is not enlisted in any large numbers, owing doubtless to his being quite over-shadowed and thrown into the background by the Jat Sikh.

Sikh Chuhras or Mazhbis.—Chuhras are sweepers by profession, and as such hold the lowest place in the social scale. The term Mazhbi has now come to be

applied to all Chuhras or sweepers who have adopted
Sikhism as their religion, but this is not the real significa-
tion of the term. The true Mazhbis are the descendants of
certain Chuhra families who were instrumental in rescuing,
at grave personal risk, the body of Guru Teg Bahadur
from the Mahomedans, and thus saving it from being
dishonoured. Guru Govind Singh, out of gratitude
for the service these Chuhra families thus rendered to his
dead father, gave them the titles of Mazhbi or the chosen,
and Rangreeta or brave, and admitted them into the fold
of Sikhism. The descendants of these particular Chuhra
families only have thus any claim to be styled Mazhbi.
The descendants of these families are however, far from
being numerous, so that the real Mazhbi is not numerous.
They have given up their old profession of sweepers and
have taken to agriculture. Inspired as they are by the
glorious traditions and history of the Khalsa, the Mazhbis
make very good soldiers. They are strong and hardy
men, and though lacking the fine well-proportioned
physique of the Jat Sikhs, they are scarcely inferior to
them in pluck and courage. The Chuhra has probably
a very large proportion of aboriginal blood in him, so
that the Mazhbi is very dark-skinned, but he has many
excellent qualities in him, and has shewn himself to be
possessed of true soldierly instincts on many occasions
when on active service. The Mazhbi is now only enlisted
for our three Punjab Pioneer regiments.

The later Chuhra converts to Sikhism are now also termed
Mazhbis, but this as has been explained is a misnomer.

However, though not genuine Mazhbis, Chuhras, who
are Sikhs by religion, make capital men for our Pioneer regiments ; and as the true Mazhbi is too small
numerically to supply all the requirements of three
pioneer battalions, it is well to encourage Sikh Chuhras
to regard themselves as Mazhbis, so that they may acquire that spirit of self-regard and pride which the
true Mazhbi feels for himself in virtue of his services
and traditions in the fold of the Khalsa. For the memory of past worth and greatness is a strong incentive to
continue such.

Sikh Tarkhans.—Tarkhans are carpenters by caste and
profession. They are intelligent and industrious men, of
whom about 20 per cent. are Sikhs by religion, the rest
being Hindu and Mahomedan. Sikh Tarkhans, if carefully recruited, could supply a fair number of good
recruits. These Sikh Tarkhans are sometimes called
Ramgharias from the fact that the Ramgharia misl was
founded by one of the class.

Kalal Sikhs or Ahluwalias.—The Kalals are by
caste and profession distillers and wine merchants on a
small scale. Twenty-five per cent. of them have now embraced Sikhism, the rest being Hindu and Mahomedan ;
the Hindus being about 50 per cent. of the whole and the
Mahomedans about 25 per cent. Sikh Kalals are often
styled Ahluwalias from the fact that the famous and important Ahluwalia misl was founded by a Kalal convert
to Sikhism. The present as well as the past Chiefs of
Kapurthala are Kalals by descent, and since the rise of

the Sikh Kalals to political prominence, they have largely given up their original profession to take to the more respectable avocations of merchandise and agriculture. The Kalals have a reputation for "enterprise, energy and obstinacy," and the Sikh Kalals make good soldiers, being of good physique and great hardihood.

As neither the Brahmin nor the Rajput have given converts in any numbers to Sikhism and have not had any affect on its history, it is unnecessary to describe them.

Khalsa Sikhs.—The Khalsa Sikh or Singh is the Sikh *par excellence*. He it is who has won empire for his religion, and who has given to the Sikh name the honour and repute it is universally held in. He is drawn from many castes, but mostly from the Punjabi Jat, to whose sturdy and independent nature the warlike and manly precepts of Guru Govind Singh naturally and strongly appealed. In the Jat Khalsa Sikh therefore, the Sikh is seen at his best and highest. Of course other castes besides the Jat have entered the Khalsa, and all of them make good soldiers, but it is the Jat Sikh or rather Jat Singh who is the truest and best embodiment of Sikhism. Jats who have adopted the other purely religious non-political Sikh sects, like the Udasi, Nanakpanthi, &c., and have not entered the fold of the Khalsa, do not make nearly such good soldiers as their brethren of the Khalsa, though doubtless, Nanakpanthi Jats, Udasi Jats, &c., are not lacking in courage. The Jat Singh is an exceptionally fine type of Asiatic. Of splendid physique, of well-proportioned and solid build, with manly and handsome

features, the Jat Singh with his sturdy self-respect and
racial pride constitutes the *beau ideal* of an Oriental soldier, inspired as he is with the knowledge that brave
deeds and proud traditions are the heritage which the past
has given into his keeping.

We shall now give a brief description of the principal
religious sects among the Sikhs. Sikhism, like every
other religious system, has in its fold a great many sects,
agreeing with each other in principle, but differing in
details. As a rule however, there is not that feeling of
acerbity and intolerance existing between the several
Sikh sects, as unfortunately does exist in the case of the
sects of most other religions. The only exception is that
of the Dhirmali Sikh sect, who are in rather bad odour
with other Sikhs.

Nanakpanthis.—Nanakpanthi means a disciple of
Nanak. It is rather a vague term, and is used indiscrimi-
nately to denote all followers of Baba Nanak. In this
wide application of the term, it is practically synonymous
with the term Sikh, and would include Sikhs of all
classes, sects, castes and tribes. But the term Nanakpanthi has now a very much more limited application, and
is used to denote those followers of Nanak who are not
also followers of the politico-religious Sikhism taught by
Guru Govind. In other words, the Nanakpanthis are a
purely religious sect, who follow the reformed Hinduism
taught by Nanak and the earlier gurus, but who are not
a political and warlike sect like the Khalsa Singhs of the
last guru. The Nanakpanthis therefore, did not have any

part in making the Sikh the dominant power in the Punjab. He does not follow the five Kakas of Govind Singh, nor does he regard devotion to steel as the first duty of man. He is not therefore a soldier by principle, instinct, and tradition. Hence recruiting from this sect is to be discouraged. But doubtless a good many excellent men could be got from among them, as, though not Singhs, they are largely Jat and Khattri by caste, and so possess to a great extent the manly and sturdy virtues of these two castes, whatever be their religious beliefs. The Nanakpanthis are also known as Mona or Muna, that is, shaven Sikhs, from the custom they have of shaving their heads excepting the usual Hindu scalplock, while the Singh of the Khalsa wears long hair. They are also known as Sahjdhari Sikhs, and in place of the *pahul* adopt the Hindu custom of drinking the water in which their guru has dipped his great toe.

Udasis.—The Udasis are a religious sect of Sikhs founded by Sri Chand, one of the sons of Nanak. They number now about 40,000, and are a purely religious body and not Khalsa Singhs. They are monastic recluses, and are in general celibates. They correspond to the Hindu jogi and the Mahomedan faquir in many ways, and like them wander about from one sacred shrine to another. They are of no military importance whatever, but are often drawn from distinctly military castes like the Jat and Khattri.

Gulabdasis.—This sect was founded by one Prithamdas, an Udasi, who owing to some differences left the Udasi sect. The name of the sect is derived from Gulabdas, a Jat disciple of Prithamdas. Gulabdas compiled the Updes Bilas, or sacred book of this sect, and was its most important teacher. They are not ascetic like the Udasis ; but, on the contrary, hold that to eat, drink and be merry is the chief end of life. They are Epicureans of the most pronounced type, and are of no value as soldiers.

Akalis or Nihangs.—The term Akali means immortal, and the sect is so called because they are worshippers of the Immortal One, or God. The Akalis are the only fanatical order of Sikhs and are Khalsa or Govindi Singhs of the most pronounced type. It is said that Govind Singh himself founded and organized this sect as a counterpoise to the Pathan Ghazi ; and whenever there was any specially dangerous or bloody task to be done, or any difficulty to be overcome requiring courage and fearlessness to a very high degree, the Akalis were usually chosen to perform it. They are also known as Nihangs or the reckless ones, though some say the word means naked. The sect is much given to the use of bhang, but abstain from flesh and liquor. They are not a numerous body, and are found mostly in the Hoshiarpore District. Like most fanatics given to the use of bhang, they are violent and unreasonable, and are subject to fits of religious frenzy, during which they are liable to be dangerous to the public peace. They were long the dread not only of their enemies, but of the other Sikhs, and under Ranjit Singh their power was very great, but since the annexation of the Punjab the sect is declining. They are rigid adherents of the five kakas prescribed by Govind Singh, but to shew their absolute devotion to the sword, they supplement the five kakas by carrying steel about their person to a very ridiculous extent. There were less than 2,000 Akalis returned during the last Census.

The last Census returns the numbers of Khalsa Sikhs at 1,870,481, but owing to the want of precision in the use of the term Sikh, Mr. Maclagan, the Punjab Census Commissioner, thinks that this number is about 30 per cent. above the real number of Khalsa Singhs in the Province. About one million and half would probably represent very approximately the real Khalsa population. The Sikhs proper, *i. e.*, Khalsa Sikhs, are found most largely in the Malwa and Manjha Sikh tracts on either side of the Sutlej, *i.e.*, in the districts of Amritsar, Ferozepore, Ludhiana, Faridkote and Nabha, where they constitute over 20 per cent. of the population ; in Patiala, Umballa, Jullunder, Kapurthalla, Lahore and Gurudaspur, where they are also found in considerable numbers and of excellent quality ; in Jhind, Hoshiarpore, Montgomery, Gujranwalla, Sialkot and Rawal Pindi, where they constitute 3 to 7 per cent. of the population. Scattered Sikh settlements are also found throughout the Punjab and even in the Pathan tracts.

In their social and domestic habits the Sikhs do not differ very materially from the Hindu. The distinguishing marks of the Khalsa Sikh are the five kakas, and the taking of the pahul. The five kakas, which were instituted by Govind Singh as necessary for all who entered the

Khalsa, are : " (1) the kes or uncut hair and unshaven
beard ; (2) the kachh or short drawers ending above the
knee ; (3) the kara or iron bangle ; (4) the khanda or
steel knife ; and (5) the kanga or comb." The pahul
has already been described. It must also be remarked
that the Singh is made, not born ; that is, a man cannot
be a Khalsa Sikh by virtue of his father having been
one. It is only when a Sikh takes the pahul and adopts
the five kakas that he becomes a Khalsa Singh. When
women are initiated and take the pahul, the dagger used
is a one-edged one, instead of a two-edged one, as in the
case of men. The taking of the pahul is prohibited
before the age of seven, and is generally deferred till the
attainment of manhood. There are no social objections
to a Khalsa Sikh marrying a Hindu woman, but she has
to go through a few minor rites. The Sikh venerates
the cow very greatly, but will eat the flesh of other
clean animals, and has no scruples in drinking spirituous
liquors or in using drugs like opium. But they will not
smoke tobacco or use it in any other way, regarding it
as utterly unclean. His clothes are by preference blue
or white, but never saffron. They burn their dead after
the Hindu fashion, and their marriage customs are much
the same as the ordinary Hindu marriage rules and
customs.

CHAPTER V.

GURKHAS.

NEPAL is bounded on the north by Tibet; on the east by Sikkim and the Darjeeling District, from both of which it is divided by the Michi River; on the south by the British Districts of Purnea, Durbhunga, Mozufferpore, Bhagulpore, Champaran and Gorakhpore; on the south-west by Oudh; and on the west by Kumaon, from which it is separated by the River Kali or Sardah. Previous to the year 1815, Nepal extended on its western side right up to the River Sutlej; but by the treaty of Segowlie, Kumaon and all the hill country west of the Kali were ceded to the E. I. Company. It is about 500 miles long and 150 miles broad, the total area being roughly about 54,000 square miles. No systematic Census of its population, which consists of a variety of races and tribes, has ever been taken, so that it is to some extent a matter of speculation; but four millions is usually regarded as a sufficiently approximate estimate.

The physical features of the country closely resemble the rest of the Himalayan regions. The southern extremity of Nepal consists of a narrow low-lying malarious tract of country, only a few hundred feet above sea-level, which is commonly known as the Terai. Beyond this is a low range of sandstone hills rising to a height of between 2,000 to 3,000 feet above the sea. Beyond this sandstone range is a long and narrow valley (or *dun* as it is known in the vernacular) about 2,500 feet high which is known as the Nepal Valley, and which is the most thickly peopled part of Nepal. Then follow the outer Himalayan ranges gradually rising to a height of about 10,000 feet, the slopes of which support a considerable population. Beyond this, again, are practically uninhabited snow-clad mountains attaining an average height of 15,000 to 18,000 feet, and which separate Nepal from Tibet.

The varying elevation of the country has given rise to a great variety of climate and vegetation, and having an abundant rainfall, the country is generally productive. Some regions, such as the Terai, are tropical in climate and vegetation ; while the higher elevations enjoy a healthy, bracing climate not unlike that of South Europe, and produce vegetation such as exists in all temperate climates. Rice, wheat, barley and Indian corn are largely grown in Nepal. Nearly all European fruit and vegetables are to be had in abundance, while essentially tropical fruit like the plantain, guava, pine-apple, flourish luxuriantly. No systematic attempt has been made to work the mineral wealth of the kingdom, but iron, copper and lead are to be had in large quantities.

Nepal has usually been divided by its people into five districts or divisions. These are (1) the Western Division known in the vernacular as the Baisi Raj Division ; (2) the Central or Sapt Gandaki Division; (3) the Eastern or

Sapt Sosi Kosiki Division; (4) the Nepal Valley; and (5) the Terai.

The Western Division, roughly speaking, extends from the River Kali on the west, to the River Relang, a tributary of the Gogra, on the east. This district was, till the Gurkha conquest about the end of the last century, divided into twenty-two hill principalities, and hence it is known to the Natives as the Baisi Raj, or country of the twenty-two states. Its inhabitants differ from the rest of the Nepal tribes in having a preponderating proportion of Aryan blood, while the Mongolian element is often scarcely traceable, the reverse being the case with the other Nepal tribes. The principal of these twenty-two states was the state of Jumla, which was regarded as suzerain among them.

The Central Division extends from the River Relang to the Trisuli Gandaki River. This district, before it was subdued by the Gurkhas, was divided into twenty-four petty states, so that it is known as the Chaobisi Raj or country of the twenty-four principalities. From the fact that seven of the principal tributaries of the Gandak flow through it, it is also known as the Sapt (or seven) Gandaki or district of the Seven Gandaks. These twenty-four states also acknowledged the Rajah of Jumla as suzerain before the Gurkha conquest. The Central Division is important as containing the original district of Gurkha, a small tract on the eastern frontier of the division, whose Rajah ultimately conquered the whole of Nepal. The chief inhabitants of Gurkha were mainly the almost purely Mongol races of Magars and Gurungs, and mixed Aryo-Mongol races known as the Khas and Thakur. There are some other races—partly aboriginal Indian—residing in Gurkha ; but the term Gurkha or Gurkhali is applied to all the inhabitants of the district of Gurkha, no matter how diverse may have been their ethnic origin. The terms Gurkha and Gurkhali are, therefore, geographical and not ethnic ; that is, they do not connote any one tribe or race, but are equally applied to distinct tribes by virtue of a common habitat in the locality known as Gurkha. The other tribes and races of Nepal, which are not connected with the district of Gurkha, are not Gurkhalis at all.

The Eastern Division, known in the vernacular as the Sapt Sosi Kosiki Division from the fact of its containing the seven principal tributaries of the River Kosi, consists of the whole of the northern part of Eastern Nepal. It is bounded on the north by Tibet, on the south by the Nepal Valley, on the east by Sikkim and the Michi River, and on the west by the Trisuli Gandaki. This district is inhabited principally by the Kirantis, Sanuwars and other tribes of Eastern Nepal.

The Nepal Valley lies immediately to the south of the Eastern Division. Originally the name Nepal was re-stricted to the Nepal Valley only, the rest of the country now going under that name being called after the names of the states of which it was comprised. It was only after the Gurkhas conquered the whole of these states that the name of the valley began to be used as the name of the whole Gurkha territory. The Nepal Valley has been from early times the homes of the Newars, Murmis and certain other tribes, and it has a varied and crowded history.

Of the Nepal Terai nothing need be said, as it does not supply a single recruit to the Army.

There can be no doubt but that from a very early period a considerable Mongolian immigration into India took place through the north-eastern passes of the Himalayas, giving rise to undoubted Mongol races like the Nagas, Jharwas, Garos, &c., on the one hand, and to certain of the tribes and races of Nepal and Bhutan on the other. The earliest known inhabitants of Nepal were therefore of the same ethnic stock as the Tartars and Chinese. The traditions of the people confirm this, as the first king of the Nepal Valley is supposed to have been one Manjushri, who came from China or rather from Manchuria. This Manjushri is still held in great regard in Nepal, and though doubtless a mythical character, his existence in Nepalese tradition helps to indicate the connection between Tartary and Nepal. Nepalese historians give a long and bewildering list of kings and dynasties which succeeded Manjushri and ruled over greater or less portions of the country in remote ages. These are all doubtless mythical, and nothing certain is known about the history of the country till a very recent period.

In addition to the early Mongol immigration into Nepal which gave rise to the bulk of its population, a second but later wave of immigration took place. This immigration was an Aryan immigration from Hindustan ; and though the exact limits of time within which it took place are not accurately ascertainable, the facts are that somewhere between the 5th century B.C. and the 12th and 13th centuries A.D., periodic Aryan inroads into Nepal took place, giving rise to the Aryan and mixed Aryan and Mongol elements in the Nepalese population. Nepalese traditions mention a long line of Aryan Chiefs from India who established themselves as rulers over parts of the country. Doubtless they are mostly mythical characters, but underlying this tradition of a succession of Rajput kings from India, is this substratum of truth, that it represents the struggle which undoubtedly took place in Nepal between two waves of immigration, one Mongoloid from Tibet, the other Aryan from India. For several centuries this struggle for mastery between the Mongol and the Aryan continued, which ultimately ended in the spiritual and intellectual supremacy of the Aryan, but which left the Mongolian element largely unassimilated ethnically and unconquered politically. The Aryans took unto themselves wives from among the Mongols, and thus a mixed race sprung up. Much the same thing happened in the case of the Aryan conquest of Nepal as happened in the case of the Norman conquest of England. The Normans, although they conquered England, in course of time were gradually absorbed into the English stock ; and though retaining a nominal supremacy, actually exercised no real sovereignty when once they had been incorporated with the English. So in the case of the Aryan conquest of Nepal. These Aryans found the country peopled by a Mongol race differing very much from them in customs, manners, blood, and speech. By their superior intelligence and not by superior courage, they contrived to gain a dominant position in the country. But this position they could only retain by identifying themselves with the Native inhabitants and coalescing with them, thus giving rise to a feeling of community and nationality between all classes.

As already stated, Nepal was not in early times under the rule of one sovereign, but consisted of a large number of petty states constantly at war with each other and torn by internal dissensions. Into the history of each of these petty states it would be futile to enter; firstly, because they have no history worthy of record, and secondly, because such traditions as exist are unreliable. A sketch of the Gurkhas, who ultimately became the masters of all these states is therefore only given.

The principality of Gurkha has no history to record prior to the 15th century A.D. All that can be said is that at some remote but historic period streams of Mongolian immigration took place into the district, giving rise to its Magar and Gurung population. At a much later period an Aryan immigration from the south resulted in calling into existence the mixed Aryan and Mongol races of the Thakurs and Khas. The Aryans converted the Magars and Gurungs to a modified Hinduism; and by virtue of their superior intelligence, acquired political and religious dominance over them, so that the mixed race became the masters of the district and gave to it its Rajahs.   As the Aryan immigrants were rarely, if ever, accompanied by their women, they intermarried with the Mongol women, so that no purely Aryan tribe exists in Nepal.

The district of Gurkha is said to derive its name in the following way.   Once upon a time there lived a guru or holy man called Guraknath or Gorakhnath or Gurkhanath. He lived in a cave in a hill in Central Nepal.   As a large number of devotees came to the holy man's cave, a village in due course sprang up on the hill near his residence, and this village naturally became known to fame as Gurkha, after the saint's name.   As the village grew in importance it became the chief town of the surrounding tract of country ; and ultimately the whole surrounding district became known as Gurkha, and its inhabitants as Gurkhas or Gurkhalis.   Thus there is both a town and a district known as Gurkha.   This guru Gorakhnath is still held in great reverence by all Gurkhas, and the battle-cry of the Gurkha is still " Guru Gorakhnath ki jai " or " victory to Guru Gorakhnath."

According to Gurkha tradition, about the end of the 15th century A.D., a Rajput Chief named Bhupal, a younger brother of the Rajah of Ujjain, left his native land owing to a quarrel with his brother, and came to Nepal, arriving at a place called Ridi in Central Nepal. He resided at different times in different districts in

Central Nepal, and during his stay in one of these—
Bhirkot—found himself blessed with two sons, who were
named Khancha and Mincha. These names are not
Aryan but Magar, so that Gurkha tradition is at fault.
These two, Khancha and Mincha, when they grew up,
conquered kingdoms for themselves in Central Nepal.
Mincha became Chief of a place called Nayakot, and his
successors extended his conquests. The sixth in descent
from Mincha was a Rajah of courage and renown known
as Kulmandan Sah. His youngest son, Yasobam Sah, was
elected Chief of one of the Chaobisi states known as
Lamzung, at the south of which was the district of Gurkha.
Yasobam in process of time slept with his fathers and was
succeeded in the Raj by his eldest son Narhari Sah, who
thus became king of Lamzung. His younger brother,
Drabiya Sah, not content with a subordinate position,
and being an able and ambitious man, left Lamzung to
try his fortune elsewhere. He therefore went to Gurkha
and resided there in an unostentatious manner for some
time. He occupied his time in quietly gaining the
confidence of its inhabitants, and then raising a revolt,
overthrew the reigning Chief of Gurkha and installed
himself as Rajah. This is supposed to have been in the
year 1599.

The Gurkha career of conquest may be said to have
begun from the middle of the last century. Narbu-
pal Sah, eighth in descent from Drabiya Sah, invaded
the Nepal Valley in 1736. He was defeated and returned
to Gurkha. He was succeeded in 1742 by his son

Prithwi Narayan Sah, then only 12 years old. The boy grew into an able, ambitious and brave man, a capable general and diplomat ; and Prithwi Narayan Sah is the greatest king of the Gurkhas, who raised them to be the dominant race in Nepal. He began his career of conquest by an invasion of the Nepal Valley, but was as unsuccessful as his father, though both he and his troops shewed splendid courage. After his failure in the Nepal Valley, he directed his attention to other surrounding states, and quickly both by stratagem and by fighting, brought several of them into subjection. In 1765 he again invaded the Nepal Valley, but was again utterly defeated in two pitched battles by its Newar inhabitants. Nothing daunted by his failures, he continued his endeavours, and by treachery obtained possession of a part of the valley. In 1768 he seized Khatmandu—also by treachery—and after four years of incessant fighting, during which he was defeated as often as he was victorious, Prithwi Narayan by his determination and perseverance subdued the whole valley with its Newar and Murmi population. The Newars in this struggle displayed great courage in their resistance to the Gurkhas, who soiled their triumph by many barbarities. Having become master of the valley, Prithwi removed his capital to Khatmandu which has ever since remained the capital of the Gurkha kingdom. His next enterprise was the subjugation of the tribes lying to the west and north-east of his dominions, but was only partially successful. He died in 1775 after an eventful, and in many respects great, reign of 33 years.

He was succeeded by his son Pratap Simha Sah, who attempted the conquest of Sikkim, but failed in the attempt. The Gurkhas were defeated in several battles by the Sikkim Rajah, and had in consequence to temporarily abandon a part of their newly acquired territories to the east. However, the Gurkhas ultimately regained all that they had lost, as in the year 1776 they again attacked Sikkim and utterly defeated its Rajah at the Battle of Chinepore.

In 1776 Ran Bahadur Sah, his infant son, succeeded to the guddi. During his infancy his uncle, Bahadur Sah, became regent. Bahadur Sah, a man of ability, determined to continue the Gurkha conquests, and directed his attention and energies to the subjugation of the Chaobisi principalities. To gain his ends he gained over the Rajah of Palpa—one of the Chaobisi states—to his side, agreeing to a division of the spoils as a return for his assistance. The Gurkha-Palpa alliance resulted in the subjugation of nearly all the Chaobisi states, the Gurkhas keeping the lion's share of the spoils for themselves. Eastward, the Gurkha arms, under their General Saroop Simha, were equally successful, and the whole of the Limbu and Rai country in Eastern Nepal was brought under Gurkha rule. For a time Sikkim also fell before their victorious arms, and Tibet also came in for a share of their attention. In consequence of the Gurkha invasion of Tibet, the Chinese government sent a strong army through Tibet into Nepal which totally defeated the Gurkhas in the year 1792. In 1793 Kumaon fell into their hands, and in the succeeding year Garhwal was utterly over-run. The permanent occupation of Garhwal, however, did not take place till some years later.

Bahadur Sah, the regent, who had so ably conducted Gurkha affairs, was removed and shortly after beheaded by his nephew, Ran Bahadur Sah, on his attaining age. Ran Bahadur committed great atrocities. In 1800 he was obliged to abdicate, being succeeded by his infant and illegitimate son, Jirban Judda Bikram Sah. Ran Bahadur Sah, after a few years' exile in India, returned to Nepal and played a conspicuous, though not reputable, part in Gurkha history till his death in 1807. In the same year the Rajah of Palpa, the sole remaining Chief of the Chaobisi raj, was reduced to subjection by the Gurkhas under the Gurkha general, Amar Sing Thapa.

Of the Gurkha War with the English little need be said, as it is so well known. Suffice it to say that the Gurkhas displayed brilliant courage, and amply justified their title to be regarded as among the finest fighting races in the world. After the peace of Segowli the Gurkhas gave up all their conquests to the west of the Kali River, which were ceded to England. At the same time the limits of the Gurkha kingdom were fixed between the rivers Kali and Michi on the west and east respectively.

Since the peace of Segowli, the relations of the Nepal Durbar with the British Indian Government have been most cordial. They offered to assist us in the Sikh War, and the services they rendered during the Mutiny are matters of history. The only other important event in recent Gurkha history is the second Tibetan War in 1854, which ended entirely in favour of the Gurkhas.

It will thus be seen that the Gurkhas enter upon the stage of history as a dominant military race only for the past one hundred and fifty years, prior to which they were only one of a large number of petty peoples occupying Central Nepal.

The Gurkhas are essentially a phlegmatic race, lacking in sentiment and emotion. And it is well for them that they are, as it is perhaps partly because of this that they make such excellent soldiers. It is but a truism to say that unemotional and practical minds are far more collected in moments of difficulty and danger than those otherwise endowed ; and few qualities are so valuable in the soldier as that of keeping cool in the heat of battle. All emotional and imaginative peoples—the Italians, Spanish, French and Greeks for example,—however brave and fearless they may be, are peculiarly apt to that excitement in the heat of battle, which is so liable to lead to loss of mental and volitional power, and hence to loss of intelligent and deliberate method in war. Colder blooded, less imaginative, and less emotional races like the English are, on the other hand, not so liable to that dangerous excitability, which, by getting the better of will and intellect, is so prone to lead to disaster in war. In this respect the unemotional and unsentimental Gurkha is much like the English ; and, like them, he is cool when in battle. And this is so not so much from any

conscious effort on his part to be so, but because his
nature and temperament are so.

But it must not be supposed that because he is cold
and sluggish by temperament, he is therefore unable
to warm to the stern business of war when occasion
requires. But his warmth is the warmth of enthusiasm,
not of excitability ; and this makes all the difference in
the world. What is often called enthusiasm is often
really excitement, but the two are far from being the
same. The history of the Indian army is full of the
many dashing deeds of arms of which the Gurkha
is the hero ; and though perhaps he does not possess the
élan of the Pathan, he has more dogged tenacity in his
composition, which in the long run, is often of more
value in the depressing business of war than fits of
ephemeral emotion and elation.

There is plenty of hearty cheerfulness about the Gurkhas, who feel a very real zest in life (as indeed all
healthy races should do) ; and they are remarkably
free from that mawkish and fault-finding spirit which
is ever bemoaning and groaning at the ills of life.
They regard everything, good and evil alike, with a
certain good humoured nonchalance, which checks any
tendency to grumble and fret. He has not got a frac-
tion of the conceit—miscalled self-respect—which spoils
some good fighting material in India ; and the discom-
forts and hardships of war do not spoil his cheery good
humour.

The following are the principal tribes inhabiting Nepal.

Khas.—As has already ·been said, the population of Nepal belongs to two great ethnic stocks, *viz.*, the Mongolian and the Aryan. The former, and the preponderating race, found its way into Nepal from Tibet, while the latter was driven into Nepal from India. The former were a fierce race of barbarians, the latter an intelligent and civilized race.

The Khas are the race resulting from the fusion of these two ethnic elements in the Nepalese population. That successive waves of Brahman and Rajput immigration into Nepal took place from very early times is certain ; and though these Brahman and Rajput immigrants formed at first only a small minority of the population, their superior intelligence and superior civilization enabled them to acquire a spiritual and intellectual supremacy over the ignorant and barbarous Mongol races of the country. This Aryan immigration was very large in Western Nepal, and thus the population of Western Nepal is more largely Aryan than Mongol. A large immigration of Brahmans and Rajputs also took place into Central Nepal, which was the home of the Magar and Gurung, but it was not large enough to supplant the original peoples. They took wives unto themselves from among the Magars and Gurungs, converted these tribes to Hinduism, and thus a large mixed population arose to which the name Khas became attached. The name Khas is said to be derived from the word "Khasnu," which means "to fall," the race having originally sprung from the illegitimate connections of Brahman and Rajput men with Magar and Gurung females. But while the great majority of the Khas people are mixed Aryo-Mongols, the term also includes the pure descendants—termed Ektharias—of those Brahmans and Rajputs who did not enter into marriage with females of the country. The term Khas is also applied to the pure Magar and Gurung descendants of the early converts to Hinduism from those tribes. The number of Ektharias is small, as, owing to the practice of secluding their women which obtains among Brahmans and Rajputs, very few women of those castes immigrated along with the men. The Aryan immigrants were therefore obliged in the great majority of cases, to marry Magar and Gurung women.

Owing to the popular opinion that the word Khas means "fallen," the Khas are now shewing a disposition to ignore that name and to call themselves Chettris. It is doubtful however, whether the popular derivation of the term is correct. Whether correct or not, the tendency of the Khas to repudiate, if possible, that name is to be deplored for more reasons than one. They acquired their dominant position in Nepal under that name ; and so, whatever its origin, it has now attached to it a certain degree of honour and repute. Further, any disposition to connect themselves with the effete and played-out Chettris of India is a distinctly retrograde step. The Khas are acknowledged to be the dominant race in Nepal. They are of slighter and less sturdy build than the Gurung and Magar, but are more intelligent and just as warlike. They are usually taller men than either Magar or Gurung, but not so

solidly built. Their language is called Khas-kura, which
is now understood all over Nepal, though it has not supplanted the dialects of other tribes resident in the country.
It is largely Hindi with a Mongol dialect incorporated
into it. The Khas are subdivided into a large number of
tribes and clans, but it is often difficult to say which is a
tribe and which a clan. Captain Vansittart mentions
nineteen tribes which are as follows :—

(1) Adhikari.	(7) Burba.	(13) Konwar.
(2) Baniya.	(8) Burathoki.	(14) Manjhi.
(3) Basniet.	(9) Gharti.	(15) Mahat.
(4) Bandhari.	(10) Karki.	(16) Rana.
(5) Bisht.	(11) Khandka.	(17) Roka.
(6) Bohora.	(12) Khattris.	(18) Thapa.
	(19) Rawat.	

Some of these names appear as the names of tribes of
other Nepal races. It is only necessary to say of the
above tribes, that the Khattris are the offspring of Brahman males and Mongol women, and are therefore known
as Khas-Khattris. There is a species of Khas known as
Matwala Khas, who are the descendants of a Khas male
by a Magar female. He is, however, usually classed,
as he is in reality, a Magar.

Thakurs.—The Gurkha Thakurs are, like the Khas, of
mixed Aryan and Mongol blood, and the distinction
between Khas and Thakur is social and not ethnic.
They make excellent soldiers, are of quite as good stuff
as the Magar and Gurung, and far excel them in
intelligence. Their social status is high, being next only

to the Brahman, the reigning family being Thakurs. They are divided into eighteen tribes or clans of which the Sahi is the best.

Gurungs.—The Gurungs are a purely Mongol tribe with little or no Aryan blood in them. Their original habitat was in the district of Gurkha, so that they are one of the Gurkhali races. Since the Gurkha conquests they have spread to other parts of Nepal. They played a prominent and distinguished part in the wars which resulted in the supremacy of the Gurkhas, and on all occasions displayed great courage. They are Hindus by religion, but their Hinduism is largely influenced by their original faith. They are of all the Nepal tribes the least under Brahminical influence and the most recently reclaimed from primitive Lamaism, so that they are remarkably free from caste prejudices. In fact they are Hindus because, that being the religion of the dominant Khas, is the fashionable religion in Nepal. Their religious beliefs are therefore as much Buddhistic or Lamaic as Hindu. The tribe is divided into two great divisions, *viz.*, the Charjat and the Solajat, the former being the acknowledged superior. The Charjat, as the name denotes, consists of four clans known as the Ghallea, Lamchania, Lama and Ghotani, and these again are subdivided into smaller septs. The Solajat is divided into eighty-six clans. In physique and in physical endurance the Gurung is perhaps the finest of the Nepal tribes. They are strong, muscular, hardy men, somewhat taller than other Nepalese tribes, and make exceptionally fine soldiers. They have few prejudices in the matter of food and drink, eat flesh, except of course forbidden flesh, and drink both their own and European liquors freely. They are a good-natured, cheery and jovial set of men who take life with easy good humour. Owing to the Gurkha conquests, the Gurung has spread far beyond his original home. Those who have remained in their original habitat are, as a rule, far superior in every way to those who have found their way into Eastern Nepal. The reason is that the former have retained the purity of their blood, while the latter, by intermarriage with the inferior Mongoloid races of Eastern Nepal, have naturally degenerated in consequence of such admixture.

Magars.—Ethnologically the Magar and Gurung are identical, that is, both are pure or nearly pure bred Mongols. It is probable that the Magars were earlier immigrants into Central Nepal than the Gurungs. Owing to their habitat being nearer to India than that of the Gurungs, they have come more under Brahminical influences than them ; and consequently their customs, beliefs, &c., partake more of Brahmanism. It is probable also, owing to the same cause, that the mixed race of Khas, is more largely the result of Aryan and Magar than Aryan and Gurung. Magars, before their conversion from Budhism to Hinduism, partook largely of beef and other forbidden flesh. The reigning family in Nepal, though it claims to be a pure Rajput family, appears in reality to have a strain of Magar blood. The tribe is divided into six great clans—the Allea, Thapa,

Pun, Gharti, Rana and Burathoki. Of these, all except the Ghartis are nearly pure Mongols, the Ghartis having an appreciable but not large strain of Aryan blood. All six clans are capable of supplying first class recruits. The Rana clan holds the highest social status of the six. Magars are now spread all over Nepal; but like the Gurungs, those who have emigrated to Eastern Nepal have degenerated owing to the infusion of inferior blood. They should therefore be recruited from their original home in Gurkha.

Sunuwars.—They are also known as Sunpars and Mukias, the latter name being given them by their Gurkha conquerors. They are an almost purely Tibetan race, and occupy a narrow strip of country on either side of the river Sun Kosi immediately to the north of the Nepal Valley and extending right up to Tibet. Their eastern neighbours are the Rais, and their western the Gurungs. Ethnologically the Sunuwars are closely allied to the Magars and Gurungs; they correspond very much in physique, and their traditions contain many recognitions of their mutual affinity. Captain Vansittart states that " Magars, Gurungs, and Sunuwars are often called in Nepal *Duwal bandi*, or two bound together, and sometimes *Okhar Pangro*, or walnut and chestnut, the intention being to convey thereby that they are as closely related as one nut to another." In physique the Sunuwars are almost as good as Magar, Gurung or Khas, but as they are not enlisted into our service, their value as soldiers is an unknown quantity. From the fact that they are taken into the Nepalese army, it would appear that their courage is held in some repute in their own land. They are divided into three great tribes according as they are the descendants of three brothers, Jetha, Maila, and Khancha. The descendants of Jetha are divided into ten sub-clans known collectively as the Dus Thare, while whose of Maila are known as the Barra Thare. The former are mainly Buddhistic or Lamaic, but their Buddhism is being superseded by Hinduism. The Burra Thare, which is the most important of the three Sunawar clans, are Hindus, which partly accounts for their superior position in a Hindu state like Nepal.

Newars.—The Newars appear to have been the earliest Mongolian immigrants into the Nepal Valley, and there is no doubt that they have been settled there from very early times. Owing to the nearness of the Nepal Valley to India, an Aryan admixture has taken place, so that, though the Newar has as a rule very decided Mongolian features, it is not uncommon to find Newars with decided Aryan features. The language of the Newars also betrays their mixed blood, as Sanskrit is clearly traceable in its grammar and etymology. They are a race of good and sturdy physique, and in intelligence far surpass the Magar and Gurung. They are industrious agriculturists, skilful handicraftsmen and clever tradesmen. They were originally Lamaic by religion, but Hinduism has now largely superseded their primitive faith. The genius of the people is largely in the arts of peace ; and though they have in their history displayed high courage, as in

their struggle with the Gurkhas, they have never been
a pronounced military race who look on war as the only
occupation worthy of men. Newars are not now enlisted
into our Gurkha regiments ; but in the past, when recruiting was not carried out on the strict lines it is now,
many Newars were enlisted and did well, some gaining
high distinction.

Murmis.—These inhabit the eastern parts of Nepal
and the Nepal Valley. It is probable that they emigrated
into their present holdings from Bhutan. They are
almost purely Mongol by race, their features betraying
no Aryan traces. They are also known as Lamas,
Thamangs, Saiyings and Ishangs. They are Buddhistic
or Lamaic by religion and freely eat cow's flesh ; so much
so, that they do not hesitate to eat the flesh of cows that have
died from natural causes. The Gurkhas therefore speak
contemptuously of them as *Siyena Bhutias* or carrion-
eating Bhutias. They are looked down on by the other
Nepal tribes, not only because of their beef-eating propen-
sities, but because they do any menial work which comes
to hand. They are mostly agriculturists, but large
numbers earn their livelihood as coolies, and being of
excellent physique can carry great loads. They are divided
into two great branches, *viz.*, the Barathamang and the
Atharajat. The former are pure Murmis ; the latter the
mixed offspring of a Murmi by any non-Murmi. The
former are also socially superior to the latter. The
Murmis have no caste system in their midst, but now that
they are subject to the Hindu race of Gurkhalis, Hinduism

and with it caste, are gradually and insiduously working their way into their social and religious life. Their physique is of the best, and their powers of endurance great. They are not soldiers by instinct and tradition, though doubtless individual Murmis can be had who would make excellent soldiers.

Kirantis.—The term Kiranti is not restricted to any one Nepal tribe, but is a word of Hindu origin applied to a group of three closely allied tribes—the Limbus or Yak-thumbas, the Khambus and Yakkas. These last two are also known collectively as Rais, while the Limbus are sometimes known as Subahs or Suffas. These three tribes regard each other as equal in all respects. The Kirantis occupy the northern half of Eastern Nepal above the Nepal Valley, the Limbus being on the east, and the Rais on the west and south. Their country is known as Kiranta, and is bounded by the Dudkosi on the west and the Aran on the east. The Kirantis at an early period played an important part in the history of the Nepal Valley. They are of mixed Hindu-Mongol stock, the latter preponderating. They are a hardy race, warlike by instinct, and have always done well as soldiers. Their religion was Lamaism till the Gurkha conquest, when Hinduism became the tribal faith. They indulged in beef-eating till then. The word Kiranti is probably derived from the Sanskrit word Kiratha or Kirantha, which means a hunter ; and the Kirantis appear to have been so called, because in early times they lived by hunting and trading in the products of the chase, such as musk, yak tails, &c.

Limbus.—Limbuana is the name given to the tract of country between the rivers Aran and Tambar or Tamru, both tributaries of the Kosi. The people inhabiting it are called Limbus by others, and Yakthumbas (=yak hunters ?) by themselves. The Bhutias and Tibetans call them Tsang, that being the name of a district in Tibet from which they are supposed to have originally come. According to Limbu tradition they are the descendants of ten brothers who lived in Kashi or Benares, and hence Limbus also call themselves Kashi Gothras. These ten brothers decided to emigrate to the hills ; so five went direct to Nepal, while the other five went to Nepal by way of Tibet, and met their brothers. Perhaps in this tradition the people have preserved the knowledge of their dual origin, for Limbus are of mixed stock, the Mongol predominating. They fought their way to the mastership of their present holdings which are bounded on the north by Tibet, the Michi River on the east, the Nepal Valley on the south, and the Aran on the west. The Limbus were masters of this tract till subdued by the Gurkhas, who committed great atrocities in the land. On taking the oath of allegiance to the Gurkha king, their Chiefs were entrusted with considerable administrative powers in the locality. Although not recognised as a military tribe, the Limbus have often displayed many soldierly qualities. They offered a stout and gallant resistance to the Gurkhas, and those in our own service have done well.

Rais.—The Khambus and Yakkas, who are collectively known as Rais, correspond in every respect to the Lim-

bus. A Limbu can become a Rai, and a Rai a Limbu.
The term Rai was an honorific title granted to the heads
of the Khambus and Yakkas by the Gurkhas after they
swore allegiance to the Gurkhas.

CHAPTER VI.

DOGRAS.

THE Dogras are a Rajput race of Highlanders, preponderatingly Hindu by religion, who occupy so much of the hills and valleys of the Western Himalayas as are included between the Rivers Chenab and Sutlej. The term Dogra is by some held to to be derived from the Indian word "dogur" or "dugur," which means a hill or mountain, and the Dogra country is so called as the whole of it is more or less mountainous. Others again derive the word from two Sanskrit words, "do "=two, and "girath "=lake, the tract in question containing two mountain lakes of small proportions but of great natural beauty known as Man Sur and Saroin Sur. In regard to the first and more probable derivation, it is said that the Rajputs from the plains of India who emigrated to the hills and founded the Dogra principalities called themselves Dogras or hillmen to distinguish themselves from their brethren of the plains.

The Dogra country is about 150 miles long and its average breadth about 80 miles. It comprises the district of Kangra, the northern tahsils of the districts of Hoshiarpore, Gurudaspur and Sialkot, the Native states of Chamba and Mundi and the Jummu District. It is

bounded on the north by the inner and loftier ranges of
the Himalayas ; on the south by the British districts of
Sialkot, Gurudaspur, Hoshiarpur and Simla ; on the east
by the River Sutlej ; and on the west by the Chenab. The
tract of country comprised within these limits is broadly
divided into two divisions by the River Ravi. The tract
between the Chenab and Ravi, roughly corresponding
with the district of Jummu, but including parts of the
Sialkot and Gurudaspur Districts, is known as the Dugar
Circle ; while that between the Ravi and Sutlej, and
comprising the district of Kangra and parts of the Simla,
Hoshiarpur and Gurudaspur Districts and the Native
states of Chamba and Mandi, is known as the Jullundur
Circle. The former is also called the Dograth country,
and the latter the Tregrath country.

The Dogra country is in most parts fertile to a degree
and yields large quantities of various cereals and fruit ;
whilst flowers, both tropical and others indigenous to
temperate climates, flourish luxuriantly. The hills abound
in cattle of good breed, and agriculture is carried on with
intelligence and care, yielding large crops. The country
is one of great natural beauty, the scenery being at once
grand and varied.

The Dogras were for a great many centuries divided
into a number of small but brave little principalities constantly at war with each other and often with the Mahomedan invaders and rulers of India. Tradition has it
that the number of these Dogra states was twenty-two,
eleven in the Jullundur Circle and eleven in the Dugar

Circle. The earliest traditions of the race claim for it a Rajput origin, and there can be no doubt that the Dogras are ethnologically of the same blood and race as the Rajputs of the plains. The main difference between the Dogras and the Rajputs of the Punjab and Rajputana plains is, that the former, because of their comparative freedom from Mahomedan domination, have a keener sense of national pride and a higher feeling of national integrity ; while the finer and more bracing climate of their hills has given them on the whole finer physiques and clearer complexions than the plain Rajputs.

As has already been said, the Dogra country is divided into two circles or divisions by the Ravi, *viz.*, the Dugar Circle on the west, and the Jullundur Circle on the east, of that river. The history of these two tracts is to some extent distinct and hence must be treated separately.

With regard to the history of the Jullundur Circle, there can be no doubt that a few centuries anterior to the Christian era this part of the Himalayas was peopled by a tribe of Rajputs, known as Katoch Rajputs, who were driven thither, either by the hordes of Scythian invaders who at that period poured into India from the north-west, or by internal discord among the Rajputs themselves. Dogra tradition favours the latter theory as the reason for their emigration into the hills. These Katoch Rajputs claim to be descended in an unbroken line from the heroes of the Mahabharat, the story being that in the wars described in that great epic, the Katoch were obliged to fly from their homes in the plains to the hills beyond

Jullundur. Originally there was one undivided Katoch kingdom in these hills ; but internal dissensions arose in due course, and so the Katoch kingdom gradually broke up into several smaller states, eleven in number. These eleven petty states, were—

(1) Chumba.	(6) Jaswan.
(2) Nurpur.	(7) Kangra.
(3) Goler.	(8) Kotleher.
(4) Datarpur.	(9) Mandi.
(5) Siba.	(10) Suchet or Suket.
	(11) Kulu.

In their mountain fastnesses these petty Dogra principalities continued to exist for several centuries till the great Mahomedan invasions of India took place. Though often defeated and obliged to admit Mogul suzerainty, their courage, coupled with the inaccessibility of their mountains, enabled them to enjoy a practical independence of Mahomedan domination. Originally however, the Katoch kingdom was not restricted to the hills, but comprised considerable tracts of country in the plains in the modern districts of Jullundur, Hoshiarpur and Gurudaspur, the Katoch capital being at Jullundur. But as Scythian emigration continued to pour into India, the Katoches were gradually driven into the hills, and the Mahomedan conquest completed the process. But the exact period when their complete transfer to the hills took place is not known.

The history of the Dugar Circle differs from that of the Jullundur Circle in this, that it appears to have originally been founded by several small streams of Raj-

put emigration, each of which resulted in the formation
of a petty state.

But these several petty states were ultimately, towards
the end of the last century, conquered and merged into
one kingdom by the state of Jummu, which became the
most powerful among them.   There were eleven of these
petty states in the Dugar Circle, their names being:—

(1) Chamba.	(6) Chineni.
(2) Badrawar.	(7) Mankot.
(3) Bilaur.	(8) Bhuti.
(4) Kishtwar.	(9) Bindratta.
(5) Padua.	(10) Jammu.

(11) Jasrota.

Thus while the Jullundur Circle originally consisted
of one undivided kingdom which subsequently, owing to
internal dissensions, split up into eleven smaller states, the
Dugar Circle consisted originally of eleven independent
petty states, which were all subsequently amalgamated into
one kingdom under Jummu.   In point of antiquity, however, the states of the Jullundur Circle take precedence.

When the Afghan invasions of India first took place
under Mahmud of Ghuzni, the Dogras of both circles
went to the help of their Hindu brethren to oppose his
advance into India, but were defeated after a resolute resistance at Peshawar in the year A.D. 1009.
Subsequent to this they were often in conflict with the
Mahomedan invaders, but though they invariably fought
with courage, they were generally defeated.   The safe
shelter of their inaccessible hills however, enabled them to

rest fairly secure from the consequences of their defeat. It was reserved for Akbar to subjugate them ; but the wise monarch, with his well-known tolerance left them practically independent, exercising merely a nominal overlordship over them. The yoke of the Mahomedan conquest therefore, did not bear very heavily on them as it did in the case of most of the Hindu states of the plains of Hindustan. Akbar gave some of these Dogra Chiefs considerable grants of land ; while Shah Jehan had sufficient trust in their loyalty and courage to entrust them with the conduct of an expedition against the Uzbegs of the Central Asian highlands. The Dogras however, did not take their conquest tamely, and they made several attempts to throw off even the nominal authority exercised over them by the Delhi throne, but were defeated and brought into closer control by the Emperor Jehangir. On the whole the Dogras behaved with marked loyalty to their Mahomedan conquerors, who appreciated their many good qualities. Many Dogras were at various times given high and responsible positions under the Mogul Emperors. Even the fanatical Aurangzebe was able to trust the government of a difficult province like Bamian to Rajah Mandata, the Dogra Chief of Nurpur. Later on, Ahmadshah Abdalli, the Afghan conqueror, made Rajah Ghammand Chand of Kangra governor of the Jullundur Circle.

During the declining years of the Mogul Empire, the Dogras became practically an independent people, even the nominal control of the Delhi throne having vanished. They continued independent till the time of Ranjit Singh,

when they became subject to the Sikhs along with the
rest of the Punjab. They served the Sikhs loyally and
well, and did signal services for them. A great many
Dogras rose to positions of trust and distinction under the
Sikhs, notably Gulab Singh, a Dogra of the Jummu State.
Gulab Singh was made Rajah of Jummu by Ranjit Singh,
and subsequently, when the annexation of the Punjab by
the British took place, Kashmir was sold to him by the
East India Company.

In character the Dogras are shy and rather reserved,
but they are not lacking in force of character. They
have not the grit and the "go" of the better classes of
Pathans and Gurkhas, nor that vigour which characterise those two races; but they are essentially a self-
respecting people, with quiet and unflinching adherence
to what they regard as their honour, and hence they make
good soldiers. They are a law-abiding and well-behaved
race, who though rather caste-ridden and under the influence of caste prejudice, give little or no trouble either in
cantonments or in the field. They readily fling aside
their caste prejudices when the necessities of war require
that they should, and thus, what would otherwise be
a stumbling-block in the way of their enlistment is
removed. His soldierly qualities are essentially more
solid than brilliant, for while lacking in dash, he is full
of quiet and resolute courage when face to face with
danger. A simple-minded, kindly, and superstitious
people, they have the sentiment of loyalty deeply engrain-
ed in them, and are alike incapable of Pathan treachery

and Pathan brutality. Their steady and resolute, though not showy, courage, renders them very reliable soldiers, and they justly enjoy the reputation of being among the best fighting material to be found in the country. They have long been known in the history of Upper India as brave and faithful soldiers, and the sentiment of loyalty to their salt is a sort of religion with them. In physique they are not tall and muscular men like the Pathan and Sikh ; nor have they the physical vigour and sturdiness of the Gurkhas. They are somewhat slightly built men of average height, with refined and finely cut features, fair complexions and well-proportioned build. Dogra recruits however, caught young, and when there is time yet for their physical development, soon fill out to respectable proportions with liberal feeding, drill, and systematic physical exercise ; and the general appearance of a Dogra regiment leaves nothing to be desired.

For recruiting purposes, the Kangra District is now the most important, as its population, both in numbers and quality, is such as to be able to furnish a large supply of excellent material for the Native army. The majority of our Dogra recruits are thus drawn from this district. Its Dogra population is predominatingly Katoch; that is, it belongs to the clan, which, being the founder of the Dogra nationality, is acknowledged as the leading clan in the tribe. The states of Mandi and Chamba are also capable of supplying excellent recruits ; while considerable numbers are to be found in parts of the British districts of Hoshiarpur, Gurudaspur and Sialkot.

The district of Jammu and the adjoining territories, though they contain a large Dogra population, have not been exploited to anything like their full extent. Generally speaking, it may be said of Dogra recruiting grounds, that the farther away they are from the influences of civilization, the finer men do they produce, both in physique and in fighting qualities; while those in closer contact with civilization are of less sturdy stuff. It is perhaps because of the inaccessibility of their mountains, which have shut them out from too intimate a contact with the physically demoralising influences of civilization, that the Dogras as a whole, have not sunk to the same level as so many once brave and warlike races in India have sunk. For the same reason some officers are of opinion that the men of the Dograth country, owing to its comparative freedom from contact with the forces of civilization, have preserved their martial qualities in greater vigour than the men of the more advanced and civilized Tregrath country.

The only Dogra castes from which recruits should be drawn are the Brahmins and Rajputs.

Although the Dogras were originally a purely Rajput colony, it was inevitable that Brahmins should have followed in their wake when they emigrated to their new homes in the mountains. The presence of Brahmins was necessary, in order that the religious ceremonies of Hinduism might be performed, which the Rajput was not competent to perform for himself. And so it came to pass that in course of time the Dogras came to have a colony of Brahmins in their midst. These, owing to the seclusion and inaccessibility of their hills, soon lost touch with their brethren of the plains, and thus came to acquire a feeling of community distinct from all other Brahmins. They thus became differentiated from the same caste in the plains, and to form a distinct Brahminical order, which, owing to location in the Dogra country, came to be known as Dogra Brahmins. As these Brahmins began to increase and multiply—and Brahmins have a way of multiplying much more rapidly than other castes—it became evident that Brahminical, *i.e.*, priestly, duties by which to earn their livelihood, could not be found for all the constantly increasing number of Brahmins. In fact, the supply exceeded the demand for their services ; and so it became inevitable that the surplus who could not find any priestly work to do, had to take to agriculture as their vocation. Thus Dogra Brahmins, like Brahmins all over India, came to be split up into two great divisions, *viz.* (1) Brahmins, who continued to perform purely priestly functions and had never throughout their descent lowered themselves by adopting other professions as their means of livelihood ; and (2) Brahmins who had through necessity been obliged to relinquish their priestly calling and to take to other means of support, in most cases the plough.

For military purposes the priestly Brahmin is of no value whatever, and they can be safely dismissed without further remark. The agricultural Dogra Brahmin, on the other hand, makes a good soldier, despite his caste prejudices and his indolence.   But they require to be very carefully recruited, as, though but a simple and superstitious hodge, he has no small notion in regard to himself because he is a Brahmin, and he is likely to be fussy and punctilious to a degree.   The average standard of physique among them is good, and they are as a whole superior physically to the Rajput Dogra ; probably because the Brahmin contrives to get more of the loaves and fishes of life than his other co-religionists.   In fighting qualities they are decidedly inferior to the better class of Rajput Dogras, like the Mian for instance ; because Brahmins as a caste have never been soldiers either by tradition, by instinct, or by occupation.   They take to soldiering not as the Mian Dogra does, from sheer love of martial pursuits, but from necessity or from motives of gain, the good pay and prospects offered by our Native army being more than sufficient to satisfy their ambitions.

From the above it will be seen that though agricultural Dogra Brahmins are capable of furnishing good recruits, they are not, as a whole, soldiers by tradition or instinct, though it does not therefore follow that they are not capable of courage and fortitude.   If however, care be taken in recruiting from this class, there can be no doubt that it can give a fairly large supply of decidedly good material.   Pride of race is strong in all Dogras, but in the case of the Brahmin Dogra this racial pride is strengthened by Brahminical pride of birth and position; so that he is essentially a self-respecting man.

The Dogra Rajput may roughly be divided into three main divisions, *viz.* (1) upper class Rajputs, commonly termed Mians ; (2) middle class Rajputs ; and (3) lower class Rajputs, usually known as Thakurs and Rathis, but who are denied the title of Rajput by the better class of the caste.

The Mians, the highest class of Rajput Dogras, are those Rajputs who have maintained the purity of their blood and their social position intact by a strict adherence to the rules of their caste. These rules are :—

(1) Never to drive the plough.
(2) To enforce strict seclusion of their women.
(3) Never to sell their daughters by accepting money for their marriage.
(4) Never to marry into a prohibited caste, or to give their daughters in marriage to lower castes.

In early times when, owing to the want of strong and well ordered systems of government, war was almost a normal condition with the majority of semi-civilized and barbarous states, the profession of arms was not merely one of honour and repute, but one also of profit. For it enabled the soldier to enjoy, either as a right or by force, the fruits of the peaceful labours of the shepherd and the ploughman. But when in process of time, society settles down into law and order, the profession of the soldier, though it may not lose in repute, becomes more restricted. And thus with a diminishing demand for his services, the soldier finds that his profession does not help him to earn

his living, and he is perforce obliged to adopt more useful
and lucrative, if not more reputable, professions than
that of arms.   And so it was with the Rajput Dogras.
In the troubled and unsettled times through which
India had passed in bygone centuries, the Rajput Dogra
had plenty of soldierly occupation wherewith to earn
his livelihood ; but as things began to settle down,
especially under British rule, the demand for soldiers became so restricted that a large part of the Dogra Rajputs
were obliged to adopt the plough as their occupation.   Now,
as has been said, for a Mian Dogra to adopt the plough is
at once to sink him into a lower scale, and the Mian who
has not defiled his hands with the plough refuses to acknowledge him as his equal.   Or again, a Mian, blessed
with a plethora of daughters, may be compelled by circumstances to marry one or more of them into a lower caste,
and this act forever deprives him and his descendants from
being styled Mians.   In these ways, all Dogra Rajputs,
though they must have originally been of the same caste,
have now been divided up into a great variety of sub-
castes ; the Mians being those who have kept their blood
unsullied and their social position intact by a strict adherence to certain rules, while those who have not, have
sunk into a lower scale.

The Mians make by far the best soldiers of all Dogras.
Soldiering has been their hereditary occupation from time
immemorial, and they regard all other occupations as unworthy of them.   They are mostly small landowners who
employ less favoured castes to till their lands for them.

But many Mians are too poor to be able to employ labour, and so they not unfrequently plough and sow their lands by night, so as to prevent detection, which would result in their sinking into a lower grade. Their rooted aversion to agriculture and the arts of peace have brought it about that they are poor to a degree, and want of proper nourishment has tended to make them of somewhat delicate physique. But the soldierly spirit is in them undiminished, and in spite of their poverty, they maintain their martial spirit and bearing. Their pride prevents them often from admitting their poverty, and the Mian will often starve in silence rather than lower himself to the subordinate position of a husbandman. Their pride moreover, often prevents their accepting service in the infantry, the cavalry being their great desire. There are a large number of grades among the Mian. Inferior castes salute them with the salutation " Jai diya," which means, " Long live the king ;" and among themselves they use the same salutation. Mians are hence often called " Jaiakari. " It is said that the title of Mian was conferred on them by a Mogul Emperor because of the distinguished courage with which they had served the imperial throne of Delhi.

Of middle class Dogra Rajput clans there are a large number ; and these clans, again, are grouped into two classes. The better of these two classes get the salutation " Jai " only, as distinguished from the " Jai diya " accorded to the Mian. The inferior of the two classes only receive the " salaam " from their inferiors, and are hence

sometimes known as " Salaami."   Both these classes alike
supply good recruits.

The Thakur and Rathi, who are classed among the
lower class Rajputs, are Rajputs ethnologically, but not
socially ; that is, they are Rajputs by origin with a
considerable, indeed a preponderating, strain of Rajput
blood.   But they have lost their social position both by
taking to proscribed avocations and by inferior marriages.
Indeed both Thakurs and Rathis have a strain of Sudra
blood in them.   They are not styled Rajputs by the better
class of Rajputs.   The exact distinction between the Thakur and the Rathi is somewhat undefined ; but generally
speaking, the Thakhur holds a higher position than the
Rathi.   It is probable also that the distinction is geographical rather than social and ethnic ; the term Thakur
being in use in the Dogar Circle, while Rathi is applied
to the same or much the same caste in the Jullundur
Circle.

Both Thakurs and Rathis, whatever be the real distinction between them, are excellent agriculturists, steady,
industrious and plodding.   Hence they are far better off
than the Mians.   They are of better physique and of
more robust constitutions than the higher Rajputs, but
do not have the same refined and well-bred features.
In soldierly qualities they are not much inferior to the
Mian, and they make excellent soldiers.   They do not
seclude their women, nor do they abstain from widow-
marriage, two practices which irretrievably consign them
to an inferior position.   In Dogra regiments they are

freely mixed up with higher caste Dogras, and their presence does not lower the Mian or the Brahmin in his own or in each other's estimation.

The Girths, another tribe inhabiting the Kangra District, are Dogras by location, but not by blood or descent. They are low caste, but industrious agriculturists, who though of good physique, have not enough of the soldier in them to permit of their admission into the Native army. Indeed, they appear to be too well off to care to enlist.

As has been said, the Dogra colony was in its infancy not restricted to the hills. Skirting the foot of the hills they now occupy, remnants of them were left there while the majority went into the mountains. This remnant was thus cut off from the main body, and during the Mahomedan era large numbers became Mahomedan by religion. Some of these Rajputs however, clung on to Hinduism, especially in the northern parts of the districts of Sialkot and Gurudaspur. These plain Dogras, if they may be so termed, are Rajputs by blood and tradition, and are of sufficiently good social position to permit of the Mian taking a wife from among them. They are thus in a way still recognised as Dogras, and though not of such good stuff as the hill Dogra, there is still a good deal of excellent fighting material to be had from among them. They are mainly agriculturists.

The Chibbs are a clan of Dogras who have become Mahomedans, and from whom good material for the army is available in small numbers.

In their social and religious customs and practices, the Dogras are much like all other Hindu communities, except that they are more superstitious and priest-ridden than men of the plains.

———

CHAPTER VII.

JATS.

THE Jats or Juts are a race of Scythian origin whose entry into India from their original habitat in the highlands of Central and Western Asia took place at a later period than that of the Aryan immigration. It is probable that their entry into India was marked by much conflict with the earlier Aryan tribes which came into the country ; but the Jat, fresh from his bracing highlands, appears to have subdued considerable tracts previously occupied by Rajputs. It is undoubted that several of the greatest kings of early India, like Khanishka, were Jats ; and a Jat or Scythian origin for Budda is also claimed by some ethnologists. Portions of the Punjab early in the Christian era, were flourishing and powerful Jat states, and continued so till they fell victims to the superior intelligence and culture of the Aryan, the Mahomedan invaders completing their ruin. Fresh inroads of Scythian tribes forced the earlier immigrant tribes of the same stock further and further east, so that the Jat is now found distributed all over the Punjab. Mr. Ibbetson is of opinion that the Rajputs and Jats are ethnologically identical, and that the distinction between them is merely a social distinction, and not one of race ; that is to say, both belong to the same ethnic stock, the difference being that the Rajput is the social superior of the Jat. Other equally high authorities disagree with this view, and maintain that while the Rajput is Aryan, the Jat is Scythian or Turanian. But this is a merely academic question of no practical value to the soldier ; and a question moreover, which cannot be finally decided until a great deal more is discovered in regard to the early races of mankind. The question of the origin and ethnic affinities of the Jat has been very lucidly discussed by Mr. Ibbetson in the Punjab Census Report of 1881, to which we would refer those desirous of more light on the subject. The Jats are now largely found all over the Punjab, parts of Rajputana and Central India, and the western parts of the North-West Provinces. The total Jat population is about 5½ millions. The Jat recruits for the Indian army are most largely drawn from the Jat state of Bhurtpore in Rajputana, from the Jumna-Ganges Doab, and from the districts of Muttra, Delhi, Agra, Gurgaon and Hissar. These eastern Jats are much the same ethnologically as the Jats of the western half of the Punjab.

Anything like a continuous and systematic history of the Jats is impossible, as materials for the same do not exist. All that can be said in regard to their early history is that they consisted of a large number of tribes each under its own Chief. These Chiefs justified their existence in their own eyes by perpetual quarrels and wars among themselves, till they were all more or less swept away

by the Mahomedan conquest. Bhurtpore is now the only
Jat state with any pretensions to importance, and as its
Chief is looked up to by all Jats of the east as their head, a
brief sketch of its history is here given.

From early times the districts around Bhurtpore had
had a large Jat population resident in them, and they
had become notorious as robbers. They gave a great
deal of trouble to the early Mahomedan conquerors,
like Mahmud of Ghazni, Timur, and Babar, by carrying
on a system of guerilla warfare with their invading hosts.
In fact, they became in course of time a regular pest
to the Mahomedan rulers, and organized a well-planned
system of dacoity. The Jats in these parts were under
the control of several Chiefs of their own race. In
the days of Aurungzebe, one of these Jat Chiefs was a
man named Churaman, who, when the Emperor was away
in the Deccan on one of his expeditions, harassed
the imperial army by guerilla attacks. A small expedition was accordingly sent against these Jat robber communities. After several unsuccessful attempts, the fort
of Thun, the principal stronghold of Churaman, was
reduced by the Moguls through the treachery of Badan
Singh, the brother of Churaman. In return for the help
given by Badan Singh, he was installed at Deeg,
by order of the Delhi Court, as Chief of the Jats with
the title of Thakur. He held his lands as military
fiefs of the Mogul Emperor, to whom he remained loyal
during the rest of his life. He was succeeded by his
son, Suraj Mal, who removed the Jat capital to Bhurtpore,

having first killed its Jat Chief, one Khema, who was a
relative of Suraj Mal's.   Suraj Mal was a man of courage
and ability, and soon consolidated his power and organised
his territories.   He assumed the title of Rajah to increase
his importance.   He took a conspicuous part in the
rebellions and civil wars which after the death of Aurungzebe betokened the beginning of the end of the Mogul
Empire.   In 1761 Suraj Mal joined the Mahrattas in
opposing Ahmad Shah Duranni ; but disagreeing with
the Mahratta Chief as to the plan of camping to be
adopted, he withdrew his forces, amounting to 30,000
men, before the famous Battle of Panipat.   Taking advantage of the confusion consequent on the absence of a
strong central government, Suraj Mal attacked and seized
Agra, then in the hands of the Mahrattas.   Emboldened
by success, he next essayed to attack the Moguls themselves ; but while out hunting, shortly before giving battle
to the Imperial troops, he was surprised, captured, and
beheaded by a troop of Mogul cavalry.   His son, Jawahir
Singh, not knowing his father's fate, attacked the Imperial army ; but the news of Suraj Mal's death so dis-
heartened the Jats that they were easily defeated.   The
Jat defeat did not however produce any evil results for
them, as the Delhi Court was too rotten to take advantage
of their success.   Jawahir Singh therefore, who succeeded
Suraj Mal, found himself strong enough to try conclu-
sions with the neighbouring states.   In a quarrel with the
Rajput Chief of Jaipur, he was utterly defeated, but not
before inflicting very severe damage on his opponents.

Jawahir Singh was shortly after murdered at Agra, and was succeeded in turn by his brothers Rattun Singh, Naval Singh and Ranjit Singh. Under these Chiefs the Jats were implicated in nearly all the fighting which then took place. In 1803 the Rajah of Bhurtpore was given by the E. I. Co. the districts of Kishengarh, Khattowa, Rewari, Gokul and Sahar, in return for military services rendered against the Mahrattas. But this did not prevent Ranjit Singh shortly after entering into a secret alliance with Holkar; and at the Battle of Deeg the Jat troops, which were supposed to have been sent in aid of the British, were treacherously employed against them. This treachery did not prevent the utter defeat of Holkar, who was obliged to take refuge in the fort of Bhurtpore. The fort was therefore besieged by the English, but after several unsuccessful attempts to take it, the siege was abandoned. Peace was shortly after concluded, and the districts granted to them in 1803 were confirmed to them by the British Government. A period of peace ensued till 1827, when, owing to a disputed succession, Bhurtpore was again besieged by the English and reduced by Lord Combermere, who restored the rightful heir to the throne. Nothing of any great importance has since occurred in Jat history.

The Jats are of very fair physique, and their soldierly instincts are undoubtedly great. Their history has been marked by much hard fighting; and though not so sturdy as some of the races of Northern India, their claim to be regarded as good fighting material is valid. They are partly Hindu and partly Mahomedan; but the Hindu Jat whose history has been sketched above is the only one enlisted into the Hindustani regiments. Mahomedan Jats are also found in the Native army, but under other names. The Eastern Jats of Bhartpur and the surrounding districts are mainly Hindu, and it is from them that the Hindustani Jat regiments are recruited. But in the western half of the Punjab, Jats have largely taken to Mahomedanism.

The social position of the Jat is below that of the Rajput, and they cannot now intermarry; though such marriages were permitted in early times. They practise *Karewa* or widow-remarriage, which irretrievably consigns them to an inferior position in Hindu society, and they consequently rank with Gujars and Ahirs.

The Eastern Jats who supply our Jat recruits, are mainly agriculturists, and excellent ones too they are; rarely equalled and never surpassed by any class of peasantry in India for industry and skill.

CHAPTER VIII.

ABORIGINAL TRIBES.

SOME good fighting material could be had from the superior aboriginal Indian tribes were it not that they are almost invariably lacking in those moral qualities without which good physique and great capacity for endurance are incapable of producing and developing the highest instincts of the soldier. Ages of wild and constant conflict with savage beasts, and an almost equally savage conflict among themselves and with their Aryan conquerors, have implanted in them that familiarity with pain, danger, and death, which goes far to breed a certain contempt for, and indifference towards, them. But, on the other hand, centuries of subordination, of social degradation, of the knowledge that they are universally looked down upon as a degraded race, have tended to crush out that feeling of racial pride which is so necessary in a military people, and which enables them to take death with more indifference than defeat, and which regards subordination and subjection as the chiefest of the ills of life.

It has thus come about that many aboriginal tribes, which in physique and physical hardihood are inferior to none of the Indian races, are almost totally unfit for military service, because lacking in those moral and intellectual qualities which are as essential in the soldier as physical excellence.

There are however exceptions ; and though it would be absurd to place even the very best of the aboriginal races on a par as regards soldierly qualities, with the better fighting material of the Indian army, still, some of them are not incapable of furnishing a battalion or two which would be able to render useful, if not brilliant, service. It is a well-known fact that in the early days of the Bengal army, Santals were freely recruited for it, and that they did useful service ; and also that some of the aboriginal tribes in Orissa were also similarly utilized with good results. But the duties devolving on the Bengal army in those days were not so severe, nor did they demand the same amount of soldierly excellence as is required in these days, when the Indian army has to be maintained not so much as a weapon of offence and defence against semi-civilized Native states, as for a possible and probable conflict with a great European power ; and hence it would be unwise to hold that because Santals and Kols and Gonds were admitted into the Bengal army and did good service in it in days gone by, that therefore they are good enough for our Native army now, because a great deal more is required of our Native troops now than were ever required of them a century ago.

Writing of some of the aboriginal hill tribes, Sir W. W. Hunter says : " Their truthfulness, sturdy loyalty, and a certain joyous bravery, almost amounting to playfulness, appeal in a special manner to the English mind."

Scarcely a single administrator has ruled over them for any length of time without finding his heart drawn to them, and leaving on record his belief in their capabilities for good. General Briggs writes of them in much the same strain : " They are faithful, truthful, and attached to their superiors," he writes ; " ready at all times to lay down their lives for those they serve, and remarkable for their indomitable courage. These qualities have always been displayed in our service. The aborigines of the Carnatic were the sepoys of Clive and Coote. A few companies of the same stock joined the former great captain from Bombay and helped to fight the Battle of Plassey in Bengal, which laid the foundation of our Indian Empire. They have since distinguished themselves in the Corps of Pioneers and Engineers, not only in India, but in Ava, in Afghanistan, and in the celebrated defence of Jellalabad. An unjust prejudice against them grew up in the Native armies of Madras and Bombay, produced by the feelings of contempt for them existing among the Hindu and Mahomedan troops. They have no prejudices themselves ; are always ready to serve abroad and to embark on boardship ; and I believe no instance of mutiny has occurred among them."

Again, Sir W. W. Hunter writes : " Every military man who has had anything to do with the aboriginal races acknowledges that once they admit a claim on their allegiance nothing tempts them to a treacherous or disloyal act." " The fidelity to their acknowledged Chief," wrote Captain Hunter, " is very remarkable ; and so strong

is their attachment that in no situation or condition,
however desperate, can they be induced to betray him. ''
Their obedience to recognised authority is absolute ; and
Colonel Tod relates how the wife of an absent chieftain
procured for a British messenger safe conduct and hospitality through the densest forest by giving him one of her
husband's arrows as a token.   The very officers who have
had to act most sharply against them speak most strongly,
and often not without a noble regret and self-reproach,
in their favour.   " It was not war," Major Vincent Jervis
writes of the operations against the Santals in 1855. "They
did not understand yielding ; as long as their national
drums beat, the whole party would stand, and allow themselves to be shot down.   They were the most truthful set
of men I ever met."

With such high testimony in their favour, it would
perhaps be unwise to altogether shut out all the aboriginal
tribes from a career as soldiers ; and, as has been said,
there are a few aboriginal tribes which could supply a
battalion or two which would not discredit our Native
army.   The principal of such tribes are the following :—

Bhils.—Chief among the aboriginal soldierly tribes
are the Bhils.   This race inhabits large tracts of country,
almost entirely hilly and mountainous, in Rajputana and
Central India, from the Aravalli Hills in the north to the
Nerbudda in the south.   They are most numerous in what
are known as the Meywar Hill Tracts and in Sirohi, and are
also very numerous on the hills within the Rajput States
of Dungarpur, Pertabgarh, and Banswara.   In physique

they are decidedly good, as their free, vigorous, open-air life, spent largely in sport and in hunting big game, has developed nerve, muscle, and hardihood in them to a good extent. The officers commanding the two Bhil battalions, *viz.*, the Malwa and Meywar Bhil Corps, find no difficulty whatever in getting men of 5 feet 8 inches height and of proportionate girth. Men like Outram, who spent several years among the Bhils and did brilliant service among them, held them in high repute, wild, barbarous, and lawless robbers though they were. Courage they undoubtedly possess, and though treacherous with their enemies they loyally adhere to their own Chiefs whom they obey implicity. They are generally faithful to those they trust. Ignorant and superstitious they are to a degree, but scarcely more so than many of the Indian tribes who hold a higher social position. They are a jovial and good-humoured race of men, much given to drink and tobacco, plunder and sport. From time immemorial they have largely existed on the blackmail levied on merchandise passing through their mountain fastnesses, the payment of which protected merchants from being plundered and ensured their safe conduct. But times have changed with them since they were taken in hand by the British Government, and they are now largely an agricultural and pastoral people.

The relations of the British Indian Government with the Bhils commenced in 1817. In that year the Bhils first came into conflict with the East India Company, owing to a well-meant but rather unwise attempt to prematurely interfere with the rights the Bhils had enjoyed from time immemorial, to levy blackmail on all who wished to be safe from their depredations. They used to levy and realise two different taxes from the rest of the population, which were known as *rakhwali* and *bolai*. The former was an impost levied by Bhils on all non-Bhil villages in their neighbourhood, the payment of which saved all such villages from plunder. The latter was a tax levied by Bhils on all merchandise passing through their hills. If the levy was duly paid, such payment ensured safe conduct through their midst, but if not, they invariably plundered all merchandise not subjected to their exactions. The attempt of the Rana of Meywar, with the approval of the British Agent, to put a summary stop to these Bhil impositions, led to a Bhil insurrection which smouldered on for several years. In 1826 they did considerable damage to life and property in the state of Meywar. Punitive expeditions against them followed ; but ultimately, by a judicious admixture of severity and clemency, and by a kindly personal interest in them and their welfare by the British officers deputed to deal with them, they were gradually reclaimed from their habits of reckless violence and plunder to peaceful pursuits. The raising of Bhil regiments was largely instrumental in weaning them from their lawless pursuits, as it gave them honourable and lucrative employment, and at the same time raised them in the eyes of their neighbours.

Of political organisation there is little among the Bhils. In Meywar they own allegiance to certain Chiefs who claim mixed Bhil and Rajput origin. These Chiefs are the vassals of the Rana of Meywar to whom they pay a tribute which varies from Rs. 2,500 in the case of the principle of these Chiefs, to Rs. 61 in the case of the smallest. They are grouped under two classes known as the Bhumia Chiefs and the Grasia Chiefs. The following are a list of these Chiefs :—

Bhumia Chiefs.

The Rao of Jawas.

The Rao of Para.

The Rao of Madri.

The Thakur of Chani.

The Thakur of Thana.

The Thakur of Patia.

The Thakur of Sarwan.

Grasia Chiefs.

The Rao of Jura.

The Rana of Panarwa.

The Rao of Oghna.

In other Rajput states the Bhils own no allegiance to any Chief of their own race, but hold their lands as fiefs of the Rajput Chief in whose territory they live. This vassalage in the old unsettled days was rather nominal than real, and it was only after order had been securely established in the Bhil country by the British Government that their allegiance to the head of the Rajput State in which they lived was securely established.

The Bhils are Hindu by religion, but their Hinduism is of a very gross type, and consists largely in propitiating the evil spirits and the malignant godlings who, according

B, FR   10

to their ideas, are at the bottom of all human ills. Their social customs are much the same as other Hindus.

Meos.—Although the Meos claim a Rajput origin, it is almost certain that they are an aboriginal tribe but with a considerable strain of Aryan blood in them. Their habitat is the tract of country known as Mewat, comprising the districts of Alwar, Gurgaon and Bhurtpore, and parts of the Delhi District. Before the Mahomedan conquest they were Hindus by religion, but on the establishment of Islam as a dominant religion in India they readily renounced their Hinduism, and the tribe is now almost entirely Mahomedan. But their Mahomedanism is of the crudest, and they are even ignorant of many of the most elementary articles of their faith, Hinduism entering very largely into their religious ideas. Many of their social customs are still Hindu, and they retain many Hindu characteristics. They are thieves by instinct and tradition, and their history has been marked by much turbulence and disorderliness. They do not hesitate to get drunk on the slightest provocation and are far from being a reputable lot. However, they are quiet and orderly enough now, and have perforce renounced their hereditary occupation of robbery for the more honest but less showy plough. But they have not the industry to become first class agriculturists, and the tribe is on the whole a poor one.

In regard to their soldierly qualities, there can be no doubt that in days gone by the Meos took freely to military service, and that they did good service as soldiers.

But, of course, it would be absurd to class the Meo as a
first class fighting man. He has been too accustomed to
political subjection and social degredation to keep alive
in him the highest instincts of the soldier. But for all that
he is not to be lightly esteemed ; and it is suggested
that recruitment for the native artillery in Mauritius,
Straits Settlements, &c., should be prohibited from Jat
Sikhs, the better classes of Punjabi Mahomedans, and
other first class fighting material ; and that those colonies
should only be permitted to recruit from the lesser martial
castes of this country, among which races like the Bhils,
Meos, Minas, Mhers, &c., form a not unimportant factor.
These lesser castes are quite good enough for any services
that may be required of them in those small colonies ;
and it seems a waste of good material to allow several
thousands of our best fighting material to run to waste
in other lands when there is such a demand for them in
India.

Meenas.--The Meenas (or Minas) are another aboriginal race which could undoubtedly supply a large number
of good recruits. They too, have a strain of Aryan blood
in them, and their habitat is the western part of the Central
India Agency and parts of Rajputana. They number about
300,000 souls, are of good physique and sturdy constitutions, and are passionately devoted to hunting large game
and other manly pursuits. In days gone by they were, like
most of the aboriginal tribes, dacoits—dacoity being an
art in which they excelled. They are now largely agricultural, but are also largely employed as watchmen by Raj-

put families. They are enlisted in the Deoli and Erinpura Forces and have done well in it. The principal Rajput states in which they are found are Jaipur, Alwar, Meywar and Sirohi, in each of which they have considerable settlements. Originally they were the dominant race in these tracts, but were subdued by the Rajputs ; but not until after they had offered a brave and resolute resistance to the conquerors. Indeed, Rajput history is full of ghastly incidents of bloodshed and massacre brought about by the stubborn resistance offered by the Minas. Even now they not unfrequently give trouble to the Rajput Chiefs under whom they live, and there can be no doubt that they have much of the soldierly instinct in them.

Mhers or Mers.—The word Mēr or Mher is derived from the word " mer " or " meru," a hill ; so that Mēr means a hillman or highlander. The Mērs are closely related to the Minas ; indeed, it is probable that the distinction between Mēr and Meena is geographical rather than ethnic. In other words the Meena and Mēr belong to the same ethnic stock, but have come to be distinct peoples by virtue of their occupying distinct tracts of country. Mher tradition claims for them a Rajput origin, the story current among them being that they are descendants of Rajput fathers and Mina mothers. This tradition embodies a part of the truth in regard to their origin, for the Mērs have an undoubted strain of Rajput blood in them; but there can be no doubt that the preponderating racial element in them is aboriginal and not Rajput. Their habitat usually known as Mherwarra is a long and narrow range of hills near the central parts of Rajputana. In these mountain fastnesses of theirs, they had for centuries successfully resisted all attempts by Rajput Chiefs to subdue them, and Rajput dominion over them was usually more nominal than real. They are of excellent physique and hardy constitutions. There are large numbers of them in the Mherwarra Battalion, a corps which, by providing them with honourable and lucrative service, has done much to reclaim them from their previous habits of dacoity and plunder.

Moghias.—The Moghias, who inhabit parts of the Central India Agency, are a brave and warlike aboriginal tribe who have only been recently reclaimed from being a community of robbers to peaceful and industrious agriculturists. There is however, a good deal of the old Adam still in them, and they are ever spoiling for a fight whenever a pretext arises. They are hardy men, of good physique, and would doubtless be able to furnish some good recruits.

CHAPTER IX.

Fighting Races of South India.

A GREAT deal has yet to be learned in regard to the ethnology of the races, tribes, and peoples inhabiting the Southern Presidency. The more interesting peoples of Northern India have appealed to the imaginations of a large number of ethnologists, who have threshed out a great deal of the information procurable in regard to them. The sturdy and warlike races of the Punjab, Rajputana, &c., all with grand traditions to look back upon, and the representatives of once vigorous and romantic civilizations, easily attract men to their study. But the essentially commonplace Tamil and Telugu do not seem to appeal even to the sober and unimaginative ethnologist, for there is a great dearth of information in regard to Madrassi ethnology and ethnography.

However this may be, it is pretty certain that the bulk of the population of the Madras Presidency is Dravidian; that is, that they belong to a race which entered India through the passes of the North-West frontier, prior to the entrance of the Aryan settlers. Aryan immigration resulted in the Dravidian races being driven further and further south till they were confined within their present limits. The Dravidians were not originally Hindus by religion; and hence the system of caste is not indigenous to them.   But contact with the religion of a superior race like the Aryan led to their gradual conversion to Hinduism. Thus in course of time the Dravidians began to be divided up into castes like all other Hindu peoples.   The term "Dravidian" is derived from the Sanskrit word "Dravida," which was the word used by the early Aryans to designate the peoples inhabiting the southern peninsula of India.

The Dravidians form one of the group of races known collectively by the term Turanian, and thus the racial affinities of the Dravidians are not restricted to India, but extend into Asia generally.

The total population of the Madras Presidency is 36,000,000 in round numbers. Of these, over 14 millions, or nearly 40 per cent., are Tamil-speaking. Telugu is the next most largely spoken language in the province, the Telugu-speaking population numbering about $13\frac{1}{2}$ millions, or nearly $39\frac{1}{2}$ per cent. of the total population.   Mala-yalam is the language of over $2\frac{1}{2}$ millions, or $7\frac{1}{2}$ per cent. of the population.   Canarese has $1\frac{1}{2}$ million speakers, or about 4 per cent. of the total population.   Of the other languages spoken in the Presidency, Tulu is the language of about half million of the inhabitants of the South Canara District.   Kondi and Gondhi are spoken by the aboriginal tribes of those names.   Kodagu is the mother-tongue of the people of Coorg ; while the Todas have a distinct language of their own known as the Toda language.

Nearly 90 per cent., or about 32 millions of the Madras population, is Hindu by religion.   This large preponderance of the Hindu element is doubtless due to the fact that South India did not come in for anything like the full force of the Mahomedan conquest of India by the Afghans and Moguls and other Mahomedan peoples· There are less than 2½ million Mahomedans in the whole province. Nearly half the total Mahomedan population is located in Malabar.

Of the Madras population generally it may be said that their chief defects are lack of backbone and moral hardihood. They are too pliable and plastic and soft ; too prone to inertness and dependence to be capable of becoming a great people. They are not self-reliant and self-confident. If during their history they had had the good fortune to come more and deeper into contact and conflict with the Afghans and Moguls, when these fine races invaded and conquered India, their character might have been, and in all probability would have been, very considerably stiffened and hardened by such conflict. Moreover, very few of the Turanian group of races, of which the Dravidians are only one family, seem ever to have been possessed of any great moral and physical virility. They rarely come on the world's stage as great dominant races like the Semetic and Aryan, which, even in the most backward ages of their history, have shown themselves to be essentially strong peoples.

In the Madras sepoy these defects are to some extent eradicated by the discipline and associations of the Indian army. But no amount of external education can completely change fundamental and racial defects of character.

The Madras army has every reason to be proud of its past history and traditions, for they are not wanting in gallant deeds of arms second to none in the annals of the Indian army. The part the Madras sepoy has played in the past in making the history of, and in building up, the British empire in India has been a conspicuous and distinguished one. And being by far the oldest of the three presidential armies, it has every right to regard itself with a certain degree of pride. That the Madras sepoy a century ago was a very fair type of soldier there can be no doubt of. The Duke of Wellington when in India had ample opportunities of judging their soldierly qualities, and he placed them on a par with second rate European races like the Spanish and Portuguese. That even now they can exhibit many fine soldierly qualities there can be no room for doubt ; as witness the gallant defence made by the Madras Sapper Company during the recent fighting at the Malakand. But there is equally no doubt that the Madras sepoy as a whole has greatly degenerated. The usual explanation of the cause of this degeneracy invariably is that over a century of internal quiet and peace has led to the loss of the military instinct for lack of its exercise. And doubtless this represents a large part of the truth ; for the march of order and civilization which makes the preservation of life and property one of the first duties of a civilized government, must necessarily tend to destroy that instinct which leads the uncivilized to make it his first duty to learn how to defend his life and possessions.

It may be pointed out that the fighting castes of the
Madras Presidency have not received anything like the
same systematic study as the fighting races of Upper
India. And it is probable that the difficulty of obtaining
good recruits for the Madras army is due, not entirely
to the natural dearth of good fighting material there, but
also to a want of knowledge as to what castes to recruit
from. That this is the case will appear from many
considerations. For instance, it is laid down in Army
orders that the Madras army is to be recruited from
Tamils, Telugus, Mahomedans, &c. These are the vaguest
generalities, and may mean anything or nothing. No
attempt appears to have been made to ascertain and specify
what classes of Tamils or Telugus or Mahomedans are fit
to be enlisted. There are 14 millions of Tamils, but not a
tenth of them are fit to shoulder a rifle. And so with the
others. The Army order notifying the caste composition
of the Madras army would lead one to suppose that any
Tamil or Telugu or Mahomedan was eligible for enlistment, provided only that he came up to the required chest
and height measurements and was passed by the doctor.
Recruiting on this vague basis is not permitted in the
Punjab and Bengal regiments. It is not every class of
Sikh or Gurkha or Dogra, &c., that is enlisted, but only
certain specially selected classes from among them whose
military capacities have been studied and tested. The same
system of differentiation should be adopted in the case of
the Madras population, for it is a mistake to suppose that all
classes and castes of Tamils, Telugus, Mahomedans, &c., are

on a par as regards their fitness for the army. In describing the fighting castes of the Madras Presidency therefore, we have only selected those particular castes whose history and traditions entitle them to be regarded as soldiers, and no attempt has been made to describe the Tamil or the Telugu, or the Malayalam, as a whole. For the great bulk of these races are anything but soldiers.

Tamil-speaking Castes.

Tamil is the language which is most largely spoken in the districts of Chingleput, South Arcot, Salem, Coimbatore, Trichinopoly, Tanjore, Madura, and Tinnevelly; and also in parts of North Arcot and Travancore.

The most important Tamil-speaking castes for military purposes are the following :—

Kallans.—This caste, numbering in all about half-a-million, is located principally in the districts of Madura, Tanjore and Trichinopoly. In early times they were a violent and turbulent race, much given to theft and dacoity. Indeed, the name Kallan is said to be derived from the Tamil word *Kallam*, which means a thief. The Rajah of Puddakottah is head of the caste. They appear to have given a considerable amount of trouble to the Rajahs under whom they from time to time served, refusing to pay taxes or to refrain from plunder and theft. Even at the present day, theft is a common crime among them ; and in some districts, notable Trichinopoly, heads of families are obliged to employ a Kallan as a watchman, whose employment entails a moral obligation on the whole caste to refrain from depredations within the precincts of such houses. This is not unlike the practice which used to prevail at Peshawar, where every British officer was obliged to employ a Pathan to have his belongings guarded against robbery by Pathans. Should, by any mischance or mistake, a house where a Kallan is employed be robbed by any of the caste, the goods are invariably recovered and returned to the owner. The Kallans possess a certain amount of independence of character ; and though of the average height, they are of fair physique, but are anything but a good-looking lot. Though nominally Hindu by religion, their Hinduism is of the grossest, and they indulge largely in devil-worship and other equally pleasant religious occupations. They freely eat flesh—except, of course, the flesh of the cow—and have no hesitation in getting drunk when the occasion offers. They differ from other Hindus in that they go in largely for marriages between near relatives, a practice utterly repugnant to Hindus generally. The caste can undoubtedly give a fair number of good recruits to the Madras army.

Maravans.—The next most important Tamil caste is the Maravan, or Maravar, which numbers somewhat over 300,000 souls. Mr. H. A. Stuart, of the Indian Civil Service, has described them well in his Madras Census Report of 1891, and we take the liberty of quoting a few passages : "The Maravans are found chiefly in Madura and Tinnevelly, where they occupy the tracts bordering on the coast from Cape Comorin to the northern limits of the Ramnad Zamindari. The proprietor of that estate and of the great Sivaganga Zamindari are both of the caste. The

Maravans must have been one of the first of the Dravidian tribes that penetrated to the south of the peninsula, and, like the Kallans, they have been little affected by Brahmanical influence. There exists among them a picturesque tradition to the effect that in consequence of their assisting Rama in his war against the demon Ravana, that deity gratefully exclaimed in good Tamil, *maraven,* ' or ' I will never forget,' and that they have ever since been called Maravans. But with more probability the name may be connected with the word *maram,* which means killing, ferocity, bravery and the like, as pointing clearly to their unpleasant profession, that of robbing and slaying their neighbours.

" In former days they were a fierce and turbulent race, famous for their military prowess. At one time they temporarily held possession of the Pandya kingdom, and at a later date their armies gave valuable assistance to Tirumala Nayakkan. They gave the British much trouble at the end of the last century and the beginning of this ; but they are now much the same as other ryots, though perhaps somewhat more bold and lawless."

The caste mainly subsists on agriculture, and like the Kallans, though nominally Hindus, their religion is largely demon worship. They marry by preference relations, a practice which is strictly forbidden by Hindu law ; and in many other ways do not conform to Hinduism as practised in other parts of India.

Vellalas.—This is another and the largest of the Tamil-speaking castes, numbering over two millions. They are almost entirely agriculturists, that being their caste occupation. They are fairly well off, and some good recruits could be had from among them, their physique being fair and the field for selection large.

Pallis.—This is another Tamil agricultural caste, numbering over two millions. They are to be found all over the Tamil-speaking districts. They were largely employed as soldiers in days gone by.

Other Tamil-speaking military castes are the *Agamudaiyan* or *Ahambadiyan*, who number about 300,000, and who are, ethnologically, closely related to the Kallans and Maravans ; the *Ambalakkaran*, who number about 170,000 ; the *Palayakkaran*, numbering about 18,000 ; and the *Ilamagan* and *Parivaram*, each numbering about 7,000 souls. From all these castes suitable material, though not of the best, is available for the needs of the Madras army.

MALAYALAM-SPEAKING CASTES.

Malayalam is the language spoken along the Malabar Coast, in the districts of Malabar, Cochin, and Travancore.

Nayars.—Of the Malayalam-speaking castes, the Nayars are by far the most important. The total Nayar population, which is found in Malabar, is about 400,000, and they are undoubtedly one of the best fighting races to be found within the Madras Presidency. They are Dravidians, but it has come about that in the course of centuries, a great many Tamils and Telugus and other Madras castes have emigrated into the territory occupied by the Nayars, and have thus come to regard themselves, and to be regarded by others, as Nayars. These Tamil and

Telugu immigrants are not, however, real Nayars and do not come up to the standard of the genuine Malabar Nayar, who is ethnologically of a somewhat different type. Hence in recruiting it should be carefully ascertained whether any recruit is a Nayar by birth or only by location. The only Nayar subdivisions from which recruits should be taken into the Madras Army are :—

- (1) The Agattucharna Nayars numbering   ... 33,000
- (2) The Kiriyattil Nayars numbering   ... 116,000
- (3) The Parattu Charna Nayars numbering   ... 110,000

These classes have in the past played a prominent part in the history of Malabar, where their courage and soldierly qualities made them the dominant people over considerable tracts. Of the three classes mentioned above, the second and third are practically one and the same, the term Kiriyattil being used in the southern parts of Malabar, while the Parattu Charna is more in use in the northern parts of that district. The Kiriyattil are acknowledged to be the leading class among Nayars.

It is perhaps, more correct to speak of the Nayars as a tribe than as a caste, because as a matter of fact they are a collection of several distinct castes, with distinct class occupations. Thus husbandmen, artisans, traders, dhobies, &c., are all found among Nayars, which would not be the case if they were one caste.

The Nayars in days gone by occupied to the Dravidian races somewhat the same position which the Rajputs occupied to the Aryan races of India ; that is, they were a body of professional soldiers who made war their hereditary occupation. They were given lands as payment for their military services by their Chiefs ; and they held these lands as military fiefs. When not engaged in war they spent their time in agriculture and in other peaceful pursuits, but the soldier was never subordinated to these. In other words, the Nayars, for a great many centuries past, were a community of militiamen, engaged in peaceful pursuits during times of peace, but under a feudal obligation to serve as soldiers when required by their Chiefs.

The staple food of the tribe is rice, but the more wealthy members indulge in flesh of all kinds, except prohibited articles like beef ; while all freely indulge in liquor.

There is no doubt that the Nayars could supply good recruits for the Madras army, and the wonder is that they have not been more largely enlisted than they have been hitherto.

TELUGU-SPEAKING CASTES.

Telugu is the language spoken in the districts of Nellore, Kistna, Godavari, Vizagapatam, Kurnool, Cuddapah, Anantapur, and parts of Bellary, North Arcot and Ganjam. It thus occupies practically the whole of the northern limits of the Madras Presidency. The principal Telugu-speaking castes for military purposes are the following:—

Kapu or Reddi.—This is a caste of agriculturists numbering nearly 2½ millions, which in the early years of the Christian era held a predominant position in the tracts they now occupy. They attained to some civilization, as traces of ancient greatness are still discoverable in the archæological remains found within the Telugu area. But they are now a poor lot as a whole, but being a large caste, a fair number of men of good physique can be obtained.

Tottiyans.—Though the Tottiyans are Telugus they occupy tracts in the Tamil-speaking districts of Madura, Tinnevelly, Salem and Coimbatore. They number about 150,000, and are supposed to be the "descendants of poligars and soldiers of the Nayakkan kings of Viziana-gar, who conquered the Madura country about the begin-ning of the 16th century."—(*Madras Census Report,* 1891.)

Telagas or Telingas.—"The Telagas are a Telugu caste of cultivators who were formerly soldiers in the armies of the Hindu sovereigns of Telingana. This may perhaps account for the name, for it is easy to see that the Telugu soldiers might come to be regarded as the Telugus or Telagas *par excellence.*" The caste numbers about 300,000. There are still a considerable number of Telagas in the Madras army, but their farther recruitment has been stopped.

MAHOMEDANS OF MADRAS.

Although the Mahomedans of Madras are mostly con-verts from Hinduism and are hence Dravidian by blood and race, there is yet a not inconsiderable Pathan or Afghan and Mogul element in the province which is the result of the Mahomedan invasions of Southern India. These conquering Mahomedan immigrants from Upper India, in due course intermarried with the natives of the south,

B, FR   11

forcibly and by pursuasion converting a goodly number
to their own faith. The Mahomedan population of the
province is thus made up (1) of pure-blooded Dravidian converts to Islam ; (2) the pure descendants of
Afghans and Moguls who came as conquerors into the
south ; and (3) a mixed Afghan, Mogul, and Dravidian
population. The second and third of these are capable
of supplying excellent material for the Madras army. The
Mahomedans who form the bulk of the Madras cavalry
regiments are fine men in every way, while the Mahomedans of the Hyderabad Contingent, who are much the
same as those of the Madras Lancers, are also excellent.
The only pity is that the supply is not larger. Two
Mahomedan castes deserve special mention : these are the
Moplas or Mapillas, and the Labbais.

Moplas or Mapillas.—The Moplas or Mapillas of
Malabar are perhaps the best fighting material to be had
within the limits of the Madras Presidency. They are a
fairly large class, numbering about one million, their
language being Malayalam. A large number of Moplas
are to be found in the Laccadive Islands.

Ethnologically, the real Mopla differs from the rest of
the Madras population, the race representing the union of
the Dravidian and Semetic types. In the early years of
Mahomedanism and for several centuries after, there used
to be a large trade carried on between the ports of Arabia
and of the Malabar coast. It thus came about that a large
Arab population came to be located more or less perma-
nently in Malabar. The superior race soon acquired a

prominent position on the western coast ; and being an
energetic and hardworking class of traders, they acquired an amount of wealth which enabled them to exercise
much influence on their surroundings. In time these,
Arab traders intermarried with the women of the country
and thus there sprang up a mixed race, partly Arab and
partly Dravidian, which naturally inherited a good deal
of the grit and force of character possessed by one of its
components. The term Mopla or Mapilla is, strictly
speaking, only applicable to the descendants of these
Arabs and their mixed Arab and Dravidian offspring ; but
the terms are now equally applied to pure-blooded Dravidian converts to Mahomedanism on the Malabar coast.
" The word Mapilla is said to be the same as the Tamil
word meaning bridegroom or son-in-law, and to have been
applied to the Arabs who married native women, and to
the offspring of such unions."—(*Madras Census Report*,
1891.)

The Moplas are now engaged either in trade or in
agriculture. Those on the coast, where the facilities for
sea-transport are easy, are mainly traders ; while those
more in the interior are mainly agriculturists.

They are fanatical to a degree, and their fanaticism is
of a particularly unreasonable order. The Pathan is
nothing if not fanatical, but he is a pretty level-headed
specimen of the class, and takes good care that his fanaticism is only harmful to others and not to himself. No
amount of religious bigotry will induce the majority of
Pathans to risk their necks unless by so doing they have

a reasonable chance of inflicting a commensurate amount
of damage on the hated infidel. There is, in short, method
in the Pathan's fanaticism, but none in that of the Mopla
who never stops to reckon the odds. However, be their
faults what it may, there can be no doubt they would
make excellent soldiers. They are however in most cases
too well off to care to enlist. In physique they are superior to most of the Madras castes, though they do not
attain to anything like the fine physique of the Sikh and
Pathan ; nor have they the finely cut and well propor-
tioned features of the races of Upper India.

Labbais or Sonagans.—Like the Moplas, the Labbais
are Mahomedans, and like the Moplas they are the mixed
descendants of Arab traders and Native women. The
Labbais are however restricted to the eastern or Coromandel coast, while their native speech is Tamil. The
caste or community numbers about 350,000. As in the
Malabar coast, so on the Coromandel coast, Arab traders
found their way, flourished, intermarried with Native
women, and thus gave rise to a mixed Arab and Tamil
population to which the name Labbai has become attached.
They are also known as Sonagans or Arabians, Sonagan
being the Tamil name for Arabia. Although orthodox
Mahomedans they are not fanatics like the Moplas. In
past centuries they did good military service to their
chief as horse soldiers, and they are still sometimes known
as Ravuttans, the Tamil word for a cavalryman. The
community now mainly subsists on trade, fishing and pearl
diving, and a good many recruits can be had from it of

a very fair type. A large number of Labbais are the descendants of Tamils forcibly converted to Islam by Tippu Sultan.

OTHER MADRAS CASTES.

Of the other Madras castes suitable for the Native army the following are the chief :—

Bantas.—This caste, numbering about 70,000, is found in the district of South Canara on the western coast. Their native tongue is Tulu, a Dravidian dialect. The term Banta, means a soldier, and in times past they served the Tulu kings faithfully in that capacity. They have degenerated much in these days. They are now mainly agricultural.

Tiyyans.—This is a Malabar caste of Hindus who speak Malayalam. They number considerably over half-a-million. Tradition says that they are immigrants from Ceylon. Their caste profession is toddy-drawing and distilling. The caste as a whole, is fairly well off, and contains many wealthy and educated men among them. I do not think there are many of them in the Madras army, but they could undoubtedly furnish some good men.

Bedars or Beydars.—This caste is not restricted to Madras, but is also to be found in part of Mysore and in the Bombay district of Shorapore. The Bedars of Madras, are a Canarese-speaking tribe of hunters and agriculturists and occupy the district of South Canara. They number about 53,000. They are warlike by instinct and tradition, and both Hyder Ali and his son Tippu Sultan largely enlisted them into their armies, and they gave an excellent account of themselves in the wars of those two monarchs against us. They indulge largely in open-air sports like hunting, and hence are a hardy race. As compared with the generality of the Madras population, they are physically a fine race, and every effort should be made to enlist them.

Coorgs.—The Coorg population, which is Hindu in the main, is essentially warlike. They are closely related to the Nayars ; indeed, the distinction between Coorg and Nayar is geographical rather than ethnic. Coorg was an important State even so far back as the 15th century, for the Mahomedan historian Ferishta speaks of it as one of the chief states of South India. The Coorgs offered a stout and gallant resistance to Hyder Ali of Mysore ; and later on, in their short but sharp conflict with the British, again distinguished themselves by their courage. They would, undoubtedly, make good soldiers. Their language is a Dravidian dialect known as Kodagu.

CHAPTER X.

GARHWALIS.

THE word "Garhwal" is said to be derived from "garh" a fortress, and hence Garhwal means "the land of forts;" the country in question having been at one time studded with a large number of petty hill forts, the ruins of which are still to be seen. Garhwal is a mountainous district in the Himalayas forming the north-western part of the Kumaon Division of the Lieutenant-Governorship of the N.-W. P. and Oudh. Its total area is about 5,500 square miles, and its population about 350,000. Its northern limits extend right up to Tibet, its southern face being bounded by the Bijnaur or Bijnor District of the Rohilkhand Division. On the east, it is bounded by the Kumaon District of the Division of the same name; and on the west by the Dehra Dun District and the Native state of Tehri.

The physical features, climate, and productions of the Garhwal District approximate more or less closely to the rest of the Himalayan regions. The greater part of the district consists of mountain ranges of great elevation, which are confusedly intertwined among each other without any marked regularity of formation or direction. These mountain ranges are separated from each other by narrow valleys which nowhere exceed half a mile in

width ; so that cultivation within valleys, which form so
large a part of the available culturable area in all mountainous tracts, cannot be carried on very largely in Garhwal. Further north, the mountains culminate in a series
of huge and elevated peaks, none of which are less than
22,000 feet above sea-level. The principal of these peaks
is Nanda Devi, which rises to a height of 25,660 feet
above the sea. Other lofty peaks are Kamet, 25,413 feet
above sea-level; Treesool, 23,382 feet ; Doonagiri, 23,181
feet ; Badrinath, 22,900 feet ; and Kedarnath, 22,853 feet.
Through these mountain ranges several passes lead into
Tibet, the principal of which are the Mana and Nibi
passes, along which some trade is carried on betwen Garhwal and Tibet. The principal river in the district is the
Alaknanda, which by its union with the Bhagirathi goes to
form the nucleus of the Ganges. The drainage of the
whole of Garhwal falls into the Ganges. The Garhwal
Terai is popularly known as the Bhabbar.

A quarter of a century ago the greater part of the
Garhwal District lay uncultivated, and even now the
mountain slopes are capable of producing more crops
than they actually do. Owing to the absence of broad
valleys, which naturally present favourable conditions
for agriculture, and to the steepness of the hillsides,
agriculture is a matter attended with greater difficulty
than in most other parts of the Himalayas ; and demands
considerable industry and skill. Rice, wheat, and millet,
known as *manduwa* in Garhwal, are the principal food
stuffs grown. The cultivators are mainly small peasant

proprietors, who are, as compared with the Indian peasantry generally, very well off. The hill slopes are covered
with rich pasturage which supports large flocks of sheep,
goats, cows, and other useful domestic animals. The
crops produced are sufficiently large to admit of a small
export into Tibet.

Three distinct ethnic elements are to be found in the
population of Garhwal. These are (1) an Aryan Rajput
element ; (2) a Mongol element ; and (3) an aboriginal
element.

In early Hindu writings Khas appears to have been
a prefix applied to all the hill and mountainous country
from Kashmir or Khashmir on the west to the Nepal
valley on the east ; and the terms Khasiya or Khasa were
used to denote the highlanders living within those limits.
It is probable that Kashmir, Kashgarh, Kashkara, &c.
derive their names from a more or less intimate prehistoric
connection with these Khasiyas or Khasas. These Khasas
or Khasiyas were Aryan emigrants from Central Asia,
who entered India at some remote period, occupied large
tracts of country in the Punjab and in the western parts
of the N. W.-P., but were subsequently driven into the
mountain fastnesses of the Himalayas to the north, and
into the Vindhiyas on the south, by subsequent Scythian
hordes and by the early Mahomedan invaders. Garhwal
received a considerable overflow of this Aryan emigration
from the plains ; and the Khasiyas or Khasas themselves,
who are the preponderating and predominant race in
Garhwal, claim to be Rajputs from the plains who have

fallen in the social scale, because the nature of their mountain country has prevented a strict adherence to Hindu caste rules. The Khasas of Garhwal prefer to be called Rajputs, and they are generally known as such there being no doubt that they have a large proportion of Aryan Rajput blood in them.

The Mongol element in the Garhwal population entered the district from Tibet, and as a natural consequence the population of the extreme north of Garhwal abutting on Tibet is more Mongolian than Aryan. This more or less pure Mongolian people, inhabiting the extreme northern part of the district, is known as the Bhotiyas, Bhutiyas or Bhotas. The Tibetans living on the Garhwal border are known as Huniyas, but in language, features, customs, &c., Bhotiyas and Huniyas are much alike.

The Doms, Dums, or Dhooms, who are the third ethnic element in the population, are a purely aboriginal race neither Aryan nor Mongolian, whose entry into the district is quite prehistoric. They are probably of the same ethnic stock as the other aboriginal races of India. They found their way into Garhwal, and were there subdued by the Khasiyas when these entered the district. The Dhooms do all the menial work for the Khasiyas.

In addition to these three ethnic elements in the population a fourth enters, but not to any marked extent. Owing to there being several sacred shrines in Garhwal, pilgrims from India largely flock into the district for devotional purposes. Many of these pilgrims have settled down in Garhwal, giving rise to a more or less distinct community, which differs from the Khasiyas in being a purely Aryan one, while the latter have a decidedly Mongolian strain in them.

Centuries of close contact naturally resulted in a partial fusion of the Aryan and Mongolian elements in the Garhwal population. So that though the Khasiya is in the main still preponderatingly Aryan by blood and instinct, there is a sufficient strain of Mongolian blood in him to distinguish him from a pure-blooded Aryan. Indeed, it is largely due to his Mongolian blood that the Garhwali makes the good soldier he does, for it has made him into a far sturdier fellow than he would otherwise have been. Naturally also, the closer the Khasiya is to India, the more pronounced is the Aryan in him, and the less hardy is he in consequence ; while the further he is away from India and the closer to Tibet, the Aryan becomes less preponderating, and the Mongol more pronounced, much to his gain as far as soldierly qualifications are concerned.

The Bhotiyas, who occupy the extreme northern parts of the district adjoining Tibet, are preponderatingly Mongoian by blood ; and though they have an Aryan strain in them, it is not sufficient to alter their ethnic character. They themselves however, being Hindus by religion, claim a Rajput origin, which, of course, is not valid. The Bhotiya language is closely connected with the Tibetan spoken in the adjoining districts of Tibet. The number of Bhotiyas is very small, being only about 5,000. Both men and women are sturdily built and of good physique, their principal occupation being that of carriers. Hence what trade there is between Garhwal and Tibet is largely in their hands.

Garhwal has scarcely anything like history to record except till recent times. In early historic times the whole district was split up into a large number of petty states ; each state often not more than a few square miles in area and containing only a few hundred inhabitants. In the thirteenth century there were no less than fifty-two such petty states within the district, the Chiefs of which were at constant feud with each other. About the fourteenth century one Rajah Ajai Pal or Ajai Pala, Chief of Chandpur, one of the petty Garhwal states, succeeded in reducing most of the other states to subjection, and thus established the kingdom of Garhwal. This Ajai Pal is the local hero of Garhwal, and appears to have been a man of ability and force of character. The ruins of his palace at Srinagar, his capital city, are still to be seen. Ajai Pal was the founder of the Chand dynasty, which ruled over Garhwal till the Gurkha conquest early in the present century. During the sway of the Chand dynasty, Garhwal was subject to many vicissitudes, being often invaded by neighbouring hill states and sometimes by the Rohillas of Rohilkand. They were often defeated and often victorious, but the details of their petty wars are of no interest. Suffice it to say that the Garhwalis, mostly Khasiyas, often displayed devoted courage in these wars.

The Gurkha invasions of Garhwal, which have left such a deep mark on the district and its peoples, began in the year 1791 A.D. Before however the Gurkhas could reduce the state, they were called away to repel a Tibetan attack on Nepal, but not before they had so impressed the Rajah of Garhwal by their courage and prowess, as to induce him to pay an annual tribute of Rs. 25,000 to the Nepal Darbar. An agent or ambassador from Garhwal was also accredited to the Napalese Court. Further organised aggression by the Gurkhas was, by these means, stopped, but only for a time ; and a constant succession of small plundering expeditions by Gurkhas into Garhwal continued to take place, and the Garhwal border was harried till almost a barren waste. Villages were burnt, wanton destruction of life and property occurred, and all the horrors of Oriental warfare left the border almost desolate.

In 1803 the Gurkhas, under their great general Amar Sing Thapa, invaded Garhwal in force and completely overran the whole country. Pradhaman Sah, the Rajah of Garhwal, fled before the victorious Gurkhas without offering any real resistance, and took refuge in the plains with a large number of his followers. In the plains he succeeded in raising an army of about 12,000 men with which he attempted to recover his kingdom from the Gurkhas. He was however utterly defeated by the Gurkhas at the Battle of Kharbura near Dehra Doon. In the battle Pradhaman Sah was killed as well as a large number of his following.

Till the conclusion of our war with Nepal in 1815, the Gurkhas continued to rule over Garhwal; and during those twelve years they nearly ruined the country by their barbarities. They laid the country waste, destroyed property, sold as many as they could as slaves, put most of the leading Garhwal families to death, and in other ways so maltreated the unfortunate inhabitants, that the memory of Gurkha rule in Garhwal is still fresh in the minds of its people as the darkest period of their existence. At the close of the Anglo-Nepalese War in 1815, Garhwal was ceded to the East India Company, who converted it into a British district. The East India Company however generously made over a portion of Garhwal, situated to the west of the Alaknanda River and known as Tehri, to Sudarsan Sah, a descendant of Pradhaman Sah, who was living in great poverty at Dehra. Thus it is that Tehri is still a Native state under its own Chief.

Considerable diversity of opinion has existed as to the merits of the Garhwali as a soldier; many officers speaking highly of them, others as disparagingly. But on the whole the scrutiny to which he has been subjected, has been in his favour; and the Garhwali has emerged from it with a higher reputation than was held of him before. Although Garhwali history contains few records of brilliant military successes, the mere fact that they maintained their independence for many years in spite of the proximity of first-class fighting races like the Rohillas and Gurkhas, is in itself a testimony in their favour. The resistance they offered to the Rohillas was brave and spirited ; whilst their constant little wars with Kumaon, though not characterised by the highest military qualities, were nevertheless carried on with a considerable degree of courage and pertinacity. There has always been, except till very recently, a considerable proportion of Garhwalis in all Gurkha regiments, and in these they have invariably done well. Indeed, many of the smartest Gurkha officers in the Native army were not Gurkhas at all but Garhwalis. A considerable number of " Order of Merit " men have also belonged to the same race. It used to be said that the Garhwalis in the Gurkha regiments, which took part in the siege of of Delhi in 1857, did not always do well ; but this may perhaps be due to the best class of Garhwalis not always being enlisted in those days, Garhwal being then a little known region.

It may therefore safely be stated that, provided only the best castes of Garhwal are enlisted, a Garhwali battalion would be second to none in the Native army. He is a hardy man of good physique, perhaps not on the whole as sturdy as the Gurkha, but possessing a considerable degree of physical vigour and endurance. They are accustomed to hard manual labour, and the great loads they carry speak for their physical capabilities. He is a fairly intelligent man—much more so than the Gurkha—and is not so caste-ridden as the Rajputs of the plains ; but not so free from caste prejudices as the Gurkhas. . He is not perhaps a soldier by instinct and tradition like the Sikhs

and Gurkhas ; but the fighting instinct is nevertheless
latent and dormant in him, requiring only a little en-
couragement and exercise to bring it to a head. They are
quiet and orderly in disposition, easily amenable to discipline ; but wanting in the cheerful and good-humoured
nonchalance which the Gurkha generally displays in
moments of pain and sickness. He is much more liable
to be depressed by failure than the Gurkha, and has not
the same amount of grit and backbone. Nor is he, as a
rule, such a likeable individual as the Gurkha, whose
frank and cheery *bonhomie* appeals so strongly to English-
men. Nevertheless the better class of Garhwalis possess
sufficient courage and hardihood to make excellent
soldiers ; and the new 39th Garhwali Regiment has more
than realised the hopes and anticipations of those who
were instrumental in raising it.

In the Anglo-Nepalese War of 1814-15, there were
a large number of Garhwalis in the ranks of the Gurkha
army, and they can thus fairly claim a share of the honour
that fell to the Gurkha army in the brave and spirited
resistance they offered to our troops in that struggle.

They have the reputation of being honest, in so far as
abstaining from petty thefts constitutes honesty, and they
can be relied on to faithfully discharge any trust reposed
in them.

The bulk of the Garhwal population is Hindu, the
Mahomedan population being so small as to be quite in-
appreciable. Further north however, a trace of Buddhism
is observable in the religious beliefs of the people, but

not sufficient to modify their essentially Hindu character.

Polygamy is largely practised and perhaps it is not surprising that it should be so. Owing to the narrowness of the valleys in Garhwal, which necessitates a large use of the steep hill slopes for agricultural purposes, agriculture demands a great deal of care and industry. Therefore the more beasts of burden, in the shape of wives, which a man has in Garhwal, the better off he is, because the women do a large part of the field work required in agriculture. The free practice of polygamy has not tended to elevate the morality either of the men or the women. Marriage is a matter purely of business, wives being freely bought, so that there is not much affection on either side. Widows may remarry if they can, but do not hesitate to contract unlawful connections with any man willing to have them ; nor does public opinion in Garhwal seriously condemn such connections.

The food of the poorer classes consists largely of *manduwa*, dâl, and vegetables, occasionally diversified with rice. All Garhwalis eat flesh when they can afford it, forbidden flesh only being eschewed. They brew their own liquor—a sort of beer—which they consume largely ; while their large flocks and herds enable most of them to indulge in milk and its various preparations. Like most hill dwellings, the houses are built of stone, which is so plentiful in their hills, roofed over with slate. They are very dirty in person and habits, and their houses are often cess-pools. It is owing to their dirty habits that the fever known as *mahamari*—a sort of bubonic plague—is more

or less endemic in certain parts of the district. The dress
of the males consists of a lungot or lungoti worn round
the waist, and reaching down to the calves, while over it,
from the shoulders down to their legs, is thrown a loose,
long frock, usually a blanket fastened to the waist by a
kummerbund and to the shoulders by rough pins made
of wood or metal.

The language of Garhwal is a dialect closely akin to
Hindi and belongs to the Aryan group.

For recruiting purposes Garhwal has been arbitrarily
divided into two divisions, *viz.*, Upper and Lower Garhwal.
Lower Garhwal does not offer a good field for recruiting,
so that recruitment should be restricted to Upper Garhwal. The population of Northern and Central Garhwal is,
both in physique, in physical endurance, and in manly and
soldierly qualities, far ahead of those in Lower Garhwal.

The Khasas or Rajputs, as they prefer to call themselves, form the great bulk of the population. From this
tribe the following clans only should be enlisted—

Rawats.	Goshains.
Negis.	Bhists.
Thakurs.

Each of these five clans are subdivided into a number
of smaller clans or septs.

Bhotiyas are of excellent physique, but being so small
numerically are of no use for military purposes.

The advice of the Preacher to eschew evil should be
extended to Brahmans and Dhooms who should on no
account be enlisted in Garhwal.

CHAPTER XI.

HINDUSTANI MAHOMEDANS.

THE Hindustani Mahomedan recruits for the Indian army are mainly drawn from the North-Western Provinces and Oudh with the Delhi Division of the Punjab thrown in. The total Mahomedan population of the North-Western Provinces and Oudh is about six and a half millions, found chiefly and of finest quality in the districts of Saharanpur, Mozaffernagar, Meerut, Bijnor, Moradabad, Bareilly, and Lucknow. In each of these districts the Mahomedan population is over 20 per cent. of the whole. The Delhi Division, containing as it did the chief centre of Mahomedan supremacy in India, contains, as a natural consequence, some of the finest Mahomedan peoples to be found in India.

Hindustani Mahomedans may be divided into two great divisions, *viz.*—

(1) Converts from Hinduism.

(2) The descendants, more or less pure, of the original Mahomedan peoples who conquered India.

Among the first, Rajput Mahomedans, Mahomedan Jats, Kambohs, Meos or Mewatis, Tagas and Garas, afford the best field for recruitment ; and among the latter Saiyids, Shekhs, Moguls and Pathans. A brief description of each class follows :—

Rajput Mahomedans.—Although conversions to Islam from Hinduism have mainly been from the lower castes, the superior caste of Rajputs has given a not inconsiderable proportion of proselytes to the Mahomedan faith. These Rajput Mahomedans, owing to their being of good caste, of which they have every reason to be proud, prefer to retain their caste appellation of Rajputs, and do not claim to be Saiyids and Shekhs as the lower caste converts to Islam so often do. Although Rajput conversions to Islam were at first mainly by force, as time went on large conversions took place from motives of policy ; so that many Rajput clans have now both a Hindu and a Mahomedan branch. The social position of these Rajput Mahomedans is good, both among Hindus and among Mahomedans, and they can intermarry with the best class of Saiyids and Shekhs. They are called by different names in different localities. Thus, in the Delhi Division they are usually known as Ranghars or Rungurs, a term of reproach applied to them by Hindu Rajputs for their backsliding from the faith of their forefathers. They are styled Khanzadas (a term of respect) in Oudh, while Malkhana is the name they flourish under in and about Agra.

Of these Rajput Mahomedans, the Ranghars of the Delhi Division are, perhaps, the best class of Rajput Hindustani Mahomedans to be had for the Native army.

They are a turbulent lot however, who require a firm and judicious hand over them, but their soldierly qualities are of a decidedly high order. Of Rajput Mahomedans of Hindustan generally, it may be said that they make good but not first class soldiers, being orderly, amenable to discipline and of good physique. But they are not on the whole so good as the Rajput Mahomedans of the Punjab.

Kambohs.—Kambohs are not restricted to the North-Western Provinces, but are found in large numbers in the Punjab. By religion they are partly Hindu, partly Mahomedan and partly Sikh ; but no matter what their faith they are held in high repute as industrious agriculturists. In the North-Western Provinces they are found mostly in the Meerut and Agra Divisions. Their origin is rather obscure, some giving them a Persian origin, while they themselves claim to have come from the neighbourhood of Ghazni. The fact that 40 per cent. of them are Hindus and 23 per cent. Sikhs, while only 37 per cent. are Mahomedans, clearly disproves their traditional origin from a purely Mahomedan neighbourhood. Whatever their origin, the Mussulman Kambohs of Hindustan and the Punjab are able to supply a good number of recruits for the Native army.

Mahomedan Jat.—We have in a separate chapter described the Jat, so that a second description here is unnecessary, as there is little difference between the Mahomedan and Hindu Jat. The Hindu Jat is, however, on the whole a somewhat superior man.

Garas.—This tribe of Mahomedans is found mainly in the Saharanpur District of the Meerut Division, the total number being about 60,000. They are the descendants of the early converts to Islam from Hinduism and are probably Rajputs by race. They can marry with Saiyids, so that their social position is good. They make fair soldiers and are of good physique.

Tagas.—These are a comparatively small tribe numbering in all only some 30,000 souls. Of these again, only some 6,000 are Mahomedans and the rest Hindus. They are found only in the Meerut and Rohilkhund Divisions, and are supposed to represent the descendants of Brahmans, who were for some reason or other outcasted and obliged to take to agriculture   The tribe is of no consequence.

Meos or Mewatis.—These have been described under aboriginal tribes, which see.

Saiyids.—The genuine Saiyid is of Arab descent and claims to be descended from the Prophet Mahomed, through his daughter Fatima, who married Ali, the fourth Khalifa. The tradition existing among them is that they came into India with the early Mahomedan invaders like Timur, Mahmud of Ghazni, Mahomed of Ghor, &c. ; but it is probable that the true Saiyids of India are also to a certain extent the modern Indo-Arabic representatives of the early Arab invaders who came spasmodically to the Sind coast before the Afghans. Owing to the tendency of all Mahomedans to claim relationship with the Prophet many low castes converted to Islam from Hinduism freely assume the title Saiyid, so that great care should be exercised in recruiting to distinguish the genuine Saiyid from the spurious article.

In the recruiting area allotted to the Bengal army, Saiyids are most largely found in the Delhi Division, but even here they form only a very small part of the population. The last Census shews nearly two and a half million people in the North-Western Provinces and Oudh who have classed themselves as Saiyids, Shekhs, Biloch, Pathan, &c. It is hardly necessary to say that there is probably not a quarter of this number of genuine Saiyids and Shekhs, and the actual number of true Saiyids does not probably exceed a quarter of a million all told all over India. In the Punjab, in like manner, 300,000 people have returned themselves as Saiyids, mostly in the western half of the province.

The Saiyids, having come into India as conquerors, were naturally given grants of land by their Chiefs for military services rendered in subjugating the land. Hence Saiyids are mainly small landowners and not tenants, but they now generally cultivate their own lands owing to poverty. Centuries of dominance have rendered them, in their own estimation, superior to the plough, so that they are indifferent cultivators, and only cultivate their fields from necessity. Lazy to a degree, thriftless and poor, the only profession they regard as worthy of them is the profession of war. They retain to an almost ridiculous extent their pride as a conquering race, and being of good physique make capital soldiers. They are generally too proud to take service in the Infantry, but take readily to the Cavalry.

The Saiyids are divided into two great divisions. The Hasani Saiyids are the descendants of Hasan, the son of Ali and Fatima, and the Husaini Saiyids are the descendants of Husain, also the son of Ali and Fatima. They are also classified accordingly to the locality from which they originally came, *viz.*, as Baghdadi Saiyids from Baghdad, Bukhari Saiyids from Bukhara, Meshedi Saiyids from Meshed, &c.

Shekhs.—Like the true Saiyid, the true Shekh is of Arab descent, and came into India along with the early Mahomedan conquerors. As in the case of the Saiyids, so also with Shekhs, low-caste Hindu converts to Islam assume the name Shekh to elevate themselves in the social scale, but they are an utterly spurious lot. The true Shekh is not, of course, restricted to Hindustan, but from whatever locality he comes, he makes a capital soldier, but he is an indifferent cultivator, lazy, thriftless and conceited.

They claim descent from the four Khalifas Abu Bakr surnamed Sadik the faithful, Umar, surnamed Farukh, Usman and Ali. The Shekhs are therefore divided into four great divisions named after these four, *viz.*, Sadiki, the Farukhi, the Usmani and the Alvi. Ali's descendants by wives other than Fatima are called Alvis, the descent through Fatima being called Saiyids.

Moguls.—The Moguls of India claim to be descended from the Mogul conquerors who raised such a magnificent empire in India. The Moguls are a race of Tartar origin, and their Indian descendants are most largely found in the Delhi Division, but scattered colonies exist all over the Punjab and North-Western Provinces. They have degenerated much since they lost their dominant position, and being too proud or too lazy to go in heartily for agriculture, are rather poor. The Moguls in India have scarcely retained the purity of their blood which may account for their present degeneracy, but the class as a whole, is undoubtedly able to supply a number of good recruits.

Pathans.—Pathans have been treated in detail in the first chapter. It is only necessary to say that the Pathans of Hindustan, being the descendants of Pathans who followed the victorious armies of the Afghan and Mogul, possess many good fighting qualities. But their Indian residence has to a great extent impaired their martial qualities, so that they are not to be compared with the genuine Pathan.

CHAPTER XII.

RAJPUTS.

RAJPUTS are the modern Hindu non-Brahminical and more or less pure-blooded representatives of the early Aryan immigrants into India. The common idea prevalent is that they are the inhabitants of Rájputana ; but they do not form more than a small part of the population of that province. Nor are they restricted to Rájputana, but are found in large numbers from the Indus on the west down to Benares on the east. A great portion of the Rajputs of the Punjab have been converted to Mahomedanism, and have thereby lost their distinctive character as Rajputs ; and they are now not known as Rajputs but by some other names. Some of these Mahomedan Rajput clans of the Punjab have been mentioned in Chapter III ; some of the best Punjabi Mahomedan clans being nothing more than Rajput Mahomedans. But it is not with these that this chapter deals but only with the genuine Rajputs ; that is, with those clans which are the more or less pure descendants of the original Aryan immigrants into India, and which have retained Hinduism as their religion, and Hindu ideals of life and conduct as their highest good.

These genuine Rajputs or Hindu descendants of the early Aryans are not restricted to Rájputana, but are found largely all over the North-Western Provinces and Oudh.

They were not called Rajputs, or sons of kings, because they lived in Rajputana; but they gave their name to that tract of country because they conquered it and were the ruling race in it. Their original habitat in India was not Rajputana but the Punjab. As the tide of immigration continued to bring in fresh hordes of Aryans from the highlands of Central Asia, they displaced the earlier Aryan immigrants and their descendants, who were thus obliged to betake themselves farther east. In this way, in the course of several centuries, these Aryans spread right down to the eastern limits of the North-Western Provinces, but very few Aryan colonies were formed in the Deccan; so that the bulk of the population of India, south of what are popularly called Hindustan and the Punjab, is non-Aryan. These Rajputs do not appear to have occupied in pre-historic times any part of modern Rajputana, which was mainly occupied by the Bhils and other aboriginal tribes. Each separate wave of Aryan immigration most probably resulted in the formation of a distinct Aryan clan, and as internal feuds arose among them, the larger clans must have split up into two or more smaller ones. Again, whenever any number of Rajput families, for any reason, left one holding to seek fresh fields and pastures new elsewhere in India, they gradually developed into a distinct clan differentiated from all the others. In these and a great many other ways all the various Rajput clans came into existence. In process of time these Aryans, by coming into contact with the aborigines, acquired a taint of aboriginal blood, and there can be little doubt but that some Rajput clans acquired a very considerable taint. Those clans which had preserved the purity of their blood naturally looked down on those which had not.

But the Aryans were not the only race which were attracted in early times to India. The Scythians of Central Asia followed the Aryan, but a great many centuries later, and as the Jat almost supplanted the Aryan in certain parts of the Punjab, driving them south and east. As a consequence of this, large colonies of Rajputs sprang up in the south and east of the Punjab, while other parts were largely denuded of them. Immediately before the Mahomedan conquest therefore, the original Aryans were to be found most largely in the eastern parts of the Punjab, in the North-Western Provinces and Oudh, and in Rajputana and Central India. Before the Mahomedan conquest, the Aryan or Rajput clans were of course Hindu, but the energy and vigour of the new faith resulted in a large number of Aryan clans of the Punjab adopting Islam ; while as the tide of Mahomedan conquest spread, a good many of the Rajput kings of the North-Western Provinces and Oudh were obliged to quit their homes, and with their clansmen, or sections of them, carve out fresh kingdoms for themselves in tracts where the conquering Mahomedan had not yet been. The Bhil tracts and the surrounding country were well suited for this purpose, and so it came about that during the course of the Mahomedan conquest several Rajput states sprang up in Rajputana. And so also it came about that most

Rajput clans have a branch in Rajputana and a branch in the North-Western Provinces and Oudh, that in the latter province being the parent stem; while in the former province it is generally an offshoot.

The exact period when the Rajputs first began to colonise Rajputana is not determinable, but it is certain that, although prior to the 8th or 9th century A.D., there were several Rajput states flourishing in Rajputana, some of the most important of them only came into existence after the first waves of the Mahomedan conquest had split up the ancient Rajput States in the North-Western Provinces and Oudh, such as the states of Kanauj and Ajodhiya. Probably some at least of the Rajput states in Rajputana came into existence when the great Scythian immigration into the Punjab took place, during the 5th or 6th centuries B.C. This Scythian immigration, of which the Jat is now the main representative, resulted in many of the Rajput clans being driven out of their holdings, and it is probable that some of these conquered new kingdoms for themselves in Rajputana, subduing the Bhils and other aboriginal tribes.

Although from what has been said above it would appear that the Jat and Rajput are distinct races, there are many grounds for thinking that they are ethnologically one and the same, the Jat merely representing a very much later wave of immigration of the same racial stock as the Rajput. In other words, the Rajput is the modern representative of one section of a certain Central Asian race which entered

India in almost prehistoric times and acquired new racial characteristics in their new surroundings which differentiated them from the original stock from which they sprang ; while the Jat belonged to the same race, but continued on in Central Asia for a great many centuries later. When he entered India he found himself confronted by a race of men of like blood to himself, but differentiated from him by certain characteristics acquired by many centuries of existence in a new environment and amid new conditions of life.

It should, however, be stated that Mr. Ibbetson, whose opinions on these matters are entitled to the greatest weight, holds a slightly different view. While recognising the great probability of the Rajput and Jat belonging to the same ethnic stock, he holds that the distinction between them is merely social, the Rajput representing not so much an earlier, and the Jat a later, wave of immigration of the same stock ; but that the Rajput and Jat are ethnologically one, the Rajput being merely the social superior of the Jat.

The Brahmins are also the pure, or more or less pure, representatives of the early Aryans ; but they are not on that account Rajputs. There can be no doubt however, but that in the dim ages of a prehistoric past Brahmin and Rajput were the same racially, and they are so now, the Brahmin being differentiated from the Rajput by occupational and social position.

Each Rajput state and clan, and there are a large number of them, has its own history ; and Rajput history is the history of these states and clans. But there is no history to record of the Rajputs as a race. To enter into the history of these states would be quite unnecessary for our purpose ; but we would refer those who wish for information on these matters to Tod's Rajasthan which is always available.

The dominant characteristic of the Rajput is pride of blood. In fact his pride of blood borders very close on the ridiculous. Time was when his one ambition was to wield a sword ; in these peace-loving days he is generally content to toy with it. And perhaps it is well it is so. We do not however mean to assert that the Rajput has lost his soldierly qualities, but it would be idle to say that he is still the man he once was. He is much too fond of dreaming of the past achievements of his race in the arts of peace and war, but is not particularly keen to make the traditions of a great past an incentive to further effort. He dwells with pride on the achievements of his fathers, and is content to shine in their reflected glory.

But the Rajput is still a Rajput, and it would be as idle to deny that he makes a good soldier, as it would be to assert that he is still what he once was. Proud men— we mean of course pride of the genuine and true sort—know how to die ; and if a man knows that, the essentials of the true soldier are in him. For though victory and success in war depend on the capacity to inflict death, if we make a psychological analysis of the martial instinct, it will be easily found that its primary constituent is the capacity to meet death proudly, and not in the capacity to inflict it.

The Rajput does not possess this pride in its highest form, but that he does possess it to a good extent is certain.

Too much and too little have been made of the Rajput. The eulogies that have often been passed on him are a trifle indiscriminate : while his condemnation by others is equally indiscriminate. The fact is there are Rajputs and Rajputs, and it may be laid down as a rule that the purer blooded he is, and the more free he is from the taint of aboriginal blood, the better the soldier does he make. His soldierly qualities diminish as the aboriginal taint increases. It should be remembered that a good many so-called Rajput clans have a large proportion of aboriginal blood, and recruiting should be restricted to such clans as have preserved the purity of their blood intact, though of course a slight taint of poorer blood does not sensibly diminish their soldierly qualities. A good knowledge of the ethnology of the several Rajput clans is therefore a very necessary qualification in the recruiting officer for Rajputs.

The worst about the Rajput as a soldier is his tendency to be easily depressed and knocked out of tune by failure and defeat. He is brave ; he is willing to go anywhere and do anything when things are well ; he can, by discipline and example, be made to face death in a thousand grim forms ; but the dogged pertinacity, the spirit which refuses to recognise defeat, the capacity to rise above failure, are not his. But how many, except just a few of the best of the martial races of the world, possess that spirit ? The Rajput can be got to volunteer for a desperate job, a forlorn hope, a moment of mad conflict ; but the slow, steady, depressing conditions of war leave him spiritless and broken, and it is just these very slow, steady, depressing, conditions which go largely to decide its fortunes ; and they who have the grit and resolution to withstand their deadening influence win in the long run.

In short when the day is yours and things are looking square, the Rajput is your man to do your work and do it well. But when dogged and unflinching resolution in the face of depressing circumstances are required, leave him alone ; he has not the stuff for that sort of thing.

Although, in the main, the social and religious customs of the various Rajput clans are the same, each clan has customs and rites peculiar to it ; and frequently the same clan has different customs in different localities. In Rajputana, Rajputs invariably marry out of their clan. A man may marry into a lower clan, but can never give his daughter in marriage into a lower clan without loss of social position. In the North-Western Provinces and Oudh however, this rule, though generally operative, does not invariably hold good in regard to all the clans ; some being endogamous, and as a consequence hold a lower position than clans that are not. A Rajput may marry more than one lawful wife, and it is not considered a grave moral and social delinquency to contract connections with other women if he chooses. In Rajputana, the children of Rajputs by their lawful wives are termed "*asl*," or true

Rajputs, and these are the only ones who should as a rule be enlisted for our army. The illegitimate offspring of a Rajput by a Jat or Gujar woman are termed Khawaswuls, and sometimes Suretwuls. These, although called Rajputs, are not admitted on terms of perfect equality with the true Rajput, and they are not nearly such good stuff as the genuine article. They should not be recruited except very sparingly. The numerous illegitimate offspring of Rajputs by their servant women who are usually of the lowest caste should on no account be enlisted. It is easy to tell the true Rajput from the false when recruits are brought in. A true Rajput will eat along with the Khawaswul, but not out of the same dish ; he will allow him to smoke his *hookah* through his closed hand, but will not allow him to put his mouth to it. The true Rajput again, though he will eat food cooked by the progeny of a Rajput by a servant woman, will not eat along with them, nor allow him under any circumstance to smoke his *hookah*.

The farther west a Rajput is, the less is he under Brahminical influence ; the closer to Benares, the more priestridden, superstitious and punctilious is he in regard to his religious customs. All Rajputs will eat flesh (except of course forbidden flesh), and do not object to the flesh of the wild boar, though he will have nothing to do with the common domestic pig. The Rajputs of the eastern districts of the North-Western Provinces acknowledge their brethren of Oudh and western parts of the province as their social superiors ; while all the North-Western Provinces

Rajputs look up to their clansmen of Rajputana as their betters. There is no doubt that the Western Rajputs make far better soldiers than the eastern; and the reason is to be found in the fact that the former is far more pure blooded than the latter.

There are a large number of. Rajput clans, most of which are divided into two branches, one resident in Rajputana, and the other in the North-Western Provinces and Oudh. A brief description of the principal clans follows :

Jadons (Rajputana).—Tod gives the pre-eminence among Rajput clans to the Jadons or Jadus or Jadubansis as they are indifferently called. They claim descent from Buddha, and ultimately from the moon, as they pride in calling themselves of lunar origin. That the Jadons were at a very early period of their history one of the leading clans in Upper India is evident from their wide distribution and the traces of their power which are still to be found. Anterior to the Christian era, they were the rulers in and about Delhi, Muttra and the sacred shrine of Dwarka, and they appear to have met the Greek invasion with courage but not with much success. In the present day they are the ruling race in the small Rajput state of Karauli, while a sept of the clan known as the Bhattis are paramount in Jaisalmere. The total Jadon population of Rajputana is only 55,000, of which number 16,000 are in Marwar, 9,000 in Jaipur, 8,000 in Bikanir, 9,000 in Jaisalmere, and only 3,000 in Karauli.

The Bhattis, who form a large part of the population of certain parts of the Punjab, are undoubtedly related ethnologically to the Jadon, but have now overshadowed the parent stem by their numerical importance.

Jadons are men of good physique, clean in their habits and person, and smart-looking.

Jadons (N.-W. P.).—In the North-Western Provinces they are chiefly found in the Mathura, Agra and Aligarh Districts. They are subdivided into two branches, one of which is exogamous and the other endogamous. The latter is the social inferior of the former, the men of which prefer to call themselves Jadubansis to distinguish themselves from their inferior relatives. They make good soldiers when carefully recruited, and may freely be enlisted into our Rajput regiments.

Gahlot or Sisodiya (Rajputana).—The Gahlots are the ruling clan in Meywar or Udaipur, the Maharana of which is acknowledged to be the chief of the Rajput royalties. The total Gahlot population of Rajputana is about 42,000, of which 32,000 are located in Meywar itself. They are also and now more commonly known as Sisodiya Rajputs, that being the name of the principal Gahlot sept. In fact, of the total Gahlot population of Rajputana, nearly 40,000 are Sisodiyas ; so that the two terms may well be regarded as synonymous. Of the very early history of the Gahlots there is little more than a mass of fable and tradition, and it is not till the beginning of the 8th century that we have any reliable historical data. Like many other principal Rajput clans, they claim descent from Rama, King of Ajhodiya. A descendant. of his named Bapa Rawal, in the year A.D. 728, after a long course of war and intrigue seized Chittor, and laid the foundations of the State of Udaipur. The fortress of Chittor, long so famous in the annals of Indian warfare, remained the capital of the Sisodiyas till its capture by Akbar after a desperate struggle. Throughout the Mahomedan era, they gave a very good account of themselves; and both by their valour and intelligence, were for a long period easily first amongst Rajput clans.

Gahlot (N.-W. P).—In the North-Western Provinces and Oudh the clan is more commonly known as Gahlot than Sisodiya, the preponderance of this sept not being so marked in the North Western Provinces. They are found most largely in the Agra, Mathura, Bulandshahr, Shahjahanpore, and Rai Bareilly Districts, but scattered colonies exist all over the province. The farther east they are the less warlike are they, and the best Gahlots of the North Western Provinces to recruit are all to be found in the west and centre of the province.

Rahtors (Rajputana).—The Rahtors, now the ruling clan in Jodhpur (or Marwar), Bikanir, and Kisengarh, had their original habitat in the ancient Rajput kingdom of Kanauj in Oudh. They call themselves *Suriya vansa* or descendants of the sun, and like a good many other Rajput clans, flatter themselves by claiming origin from Rama, the great Hindu mythological hero and deity. Tradition has it, and with some degree of truth, that in the 12th century, the then reigning king of Kanauj, Jai Chand by name, was defeated by the Mahomedans. His grandson or nephew, Sivaji, betook himself in consequence to the sacred city of Dwarika or Dwarka, in order to spend the residue of his days in the true old Indian fashion of prayer and contemplation, with frequent spells of sleep in between. But the surrounding country was infested with dacoits, thieves, and other pleasant mannered people ; and Sivaji having more of the man in him than to be completely fooled by the delights of the dreamy indolence miscalled contemplation which Brahminical philosophy has laid down as the highest life, found in the disturbed state of the district, something to occupy and employ his naturally active temperament. So he got together the few clansmen who had followed him, and having succeeded in freeing the district from some of its pests, he naturally began to be looked up to and respected, and ultimately he won for himself a small kingdom, which was the beginning of the now famous Rajput state of Jodhpur. When the Rahtors of Kanauj heard of the success of their clansmen in Rajputana, they emigrated largely from their original home to join their brethren, and by the end of the 14th century the Rahtor conquest of Marwar was complete. The name Jodhpur, by which the state is more commonly known, is derived from Jodha, twelfth in descent from Sivaji. As the Jodhpur state grew in importance, it threw out branches which resulted in the Rahtor states of Bikanir and Kisengarh.

The Rahtors of Rajputana are generally shorter men than those of most other Rajput clans, but are comparatively broad-chested, and hence have the appearance of being more sturdily put together than many other clans.

Like most of the superior Rajput clans, their *penchant* is for the cavalry, and only necessity obliges them to enlist in the infantry. In Bikanir, where they only number between 15,000 to 20,000, they are mostly peasant proprietors, who are too well off to care to enlist. In Kisengarh the Rahtors form a small part of the population only ; but in Jodhpur itself they probably number about 120,000. They are not so priest-ridden as the N.-W. P. Rahtors, and are certainly superior to them as fighting men.

Rahtors (N.-W. P.).—The history as a ruling race of the Rahtors of the N.-W. P. and Oudh practically ceases after the defeat by Muhammad Ghori of Jai Chand, the last Rahtor king of Kanauj. They are chiefly found in the Mainpuri, Shahjahanpur, Etah, Fatehpur, Furrakabad, Azamgarh, Agra, Moradabad, Budaon and Rai Bareilly Districts ; and also, but in much smaller numbers, in the Cawnpore, Unao, Sitapur and Baraich Districts.

The Rahtors were famous in the annals of Upper India early in the 10th century A.D., when they succeeded in wresting the ancient Rajput kingdom of Kanauj from the Tomars, another Rajput clan. They continued as the ruling race in Kanauj till their defeat by Muhammad of Ghor.

Kachhwahas (Rajputana).—The Kachhwahas are the ruling clan in the Rajput State of Jaipur, and like the Rahtors, claim to be descended from Rama. Their authentic history begins from the early years of our era

when they were the ruling clan in a part of what is now
Oudh. They remained so till their fall was brought about
by the Mahomedan conquest. About the middle of the 10th
century, Dhola Rao, a Kachhwaha prince, left his home in
Ajhodiya, and with a numerous following of his clansmen,
subdued certain of the Mina and Gujar chiefs, and founded
a state called Dhundar. Later waves of Kachhwaha
emigration from Oudh extended and completed the work
begun by Dhola Rao, and thus brought the modern Rajput
state of Jaipur into existence. The state takes its name
from Jai Singh II, the most famous of the Kachhwaha
kings, who founded the city of Jaipur. During the
Mogul sovereignty, the clan fared fairly well, Akbar
having married a Kachhwaha princess. Several of the
clan also held high appointments under the Moguls. The
most celebrated of these Kachhwaha satellites of the
Mogul emperors was Man Singh, the famous general who
in Bengal, Assam, Behar and Kabul worthily and sternly
upheld the imperial authority. Jaipur, later on, fared
badly at the hands of the Mahrattas, and the Jats of
Bhurtpore also annexed parts of Jaipur territory. The
Jaipur chiefs lost caste among their brother Rajput princes
for having given a daughter to the Mogul.

The Kachhwahas are less solidly built than the Rahtors,
and are more caste-ridden, but make good soldiers. The
Shekhawatti Rajputs are a sept of the Kachhwahas, and
derive their name from Shaikh, eleventh in descent from
Haniji, one of the early chiefs of the clan. Shaikh, who
was a younger son, being ambitious and able, conquered

for himself the tract of country round about Delhi, now occupied by the Shekhawattis.

Kachhwahas (N.-W. P.). — The Kachhwahas of Ajhodiya, although the ruling clan in their own territories, were for a long period vassals of the great Chauhan Rajput kings of Delhi. Unlike most other of the great Rajput clans, they rose considerably by the Mogul conquest; as they, both in Rajputana and the North-Western Provinces, espoused the cause of their conquerors, and thus won power and patronage. The Rajah of Rampore is now the head of the North-Western Provinces Kachhwahas. They are found chiefly in the Cawnpore, Mathura, Agra, Jalaun, Rai Bareilly and Fatehpur Districts; and in smaller numbers in the Moradabad, Sultanpur, Meerut, Sitapur, Banda, Hamirpur and Shahjahanpore Districts. They are a numerous clan, and villages occupied almost exclusively by them exist all over the western and central half of the North-Western Provinces. They are also found largely in Narwar, Gwalior, and in other parts of Central India. They are one of the best clans to recruit from.

Chauhans (Rajputana).—In Rajputana the Chauhans are the ruling clan in Kotah, Bundi, Alwar and Sirohi. For several centuries before the Mahomedan conquest they were the ruling clan in Ajmere. Prithwi Rajah, the last and most famous of the Kings of Delhi, was a son of the Rajah of Ajmere, but was adopted by the Tomara Rajput King of Delhi. Prithwi ultimately succeeded to the Delhi throne, thus uniting the Rajput states of Delhi and Ajmere.

As in the North-Western Provinces so also in Rajputana, several Chauhan septs embraced Islam, the principal of these in Rajputana being the Ladkhani, the Kaimkhani, the Amkhani, the Nimkhani, and the Kararkhani.

The total Chauhan population of Rajputana is about 56,000, located principally in the Meywar, Marwar and Udaipur states. In Alwar they number less than 6,000, in Kotah 5,000, in Sirohi 3000, and in Bundi only 2,000.

Chauhans (N.-W. P.).—Although the Chauhans do not now hold the same place among Rajput clans as they once did, historically they are one of the most important and interesting. It was a Chauhan king, Prithwi Rajah, who offered the stoutest resistance to the Mahomedans. Chauhan means " four-armed," and the clan is one of the four " fire-born " Rajput clans which were created by the god Mahadeo to destroy the demons who desecrated the sacrifices offered at his shrine in Ajmere. The other three " fire-born " clans are the Panwar or Pramar, the Solanki, and the Parihar.

They are found in large numbers in the province, but principally in the Etah, Mainpuri, Moradabad, Gonda, Fatehpur, Mathura, Budaon, Agra, Bijnor, Fyzabad, and Rai Bareilly Districts. They make excellent soldiers, but owing to several Chauhan septs having adopted Islam, the reputation of the clan among Rajputs has somewhat diminished. The principal Chauhan Mahomedan clans in the North-Western Provinces are the Baidwana, the Lowani, the Kaimkhani, the Korarwani, and the Sarwani clans. Chauhans are divided into 24 septs (excluding the Mahomedan septs enumerated above), and those of Mainpuri are acknowledged to be the bluest blooded of them all. They are not so caste-ridden as the Kachhwahas.

Panwars (Rajputana).—They are one of the four " agnicule " or fire-born clans. They were formerly called Pramaras. In early times they were a very important clan, and according to their traditions their dominion spread from the Sutlej on the east right away to the Indus and the Arabian Sea on the west. They were rulers in Chittor, but the Gahlots wrested the fortress from them. Chandra Gupta, the famous Indian king who so stoutly opposed Alexander the Great, appears to have belonged to this tribe. There does not appear to have ever been one united Pramar kingdom under one king, but there were several smaller states each with a distinct Pramar chief of its own. Some of the cities they founded are the modern Pattan, Maheshwar, Abu, and Dhar. They are mostly in Dholpore, Marwar, Meywar, and Bikanir, but they have now greatly degenerated. But there are many fine men to be found in the clan, the total population being 25,000.

Panwars (N.-W. P.).—In the North-Western Provinces they are found mostly in the Rai Bareilly, Fatehpur, Agra, Lalitpur, and Fyzabad Districts. They are divided into two great classes, *viz.*, the Dhar Panwar and the Raj Panwar, the former being the social superior of the other. Both are equally good for military purposes.

Tonwars.—This clan is really a sept of the Jadons, but having acquired political pre-eminence in early days became a separate clan. Vikramaditiya, the great king, was a Tonwar, and it was a Tonwar sovereign, Anangpal by name, who rebuilt Delhi in the 8th century. They were also predominant in Gwalior in comparatively recent times. They now number only 14,000 in Rajputana, more than half being in the Jaipur state. They are also called Tomars. In the North-Western Provinces they are found chiefly in the Shahjahanpore, Budaon, Agra, Fatehpur and Mathura Districts.

CHAPTER XIII.

MISCELLANEOUS TRIBES.

St. Thomas or Syrian Christians of Malabar.—The exact period when Christianity was first introduced into India is not clearly ascertainable ; but that it was introduced by a missionary named Thomas, early in the Christian era, is almost certain. Whether he was in reality the Doubting Apostle, as early Patristic literature makes out to be the case, is a matter of doubt. However this may be, Thomas, whoever he was, was largely successful in his proselyting mission ; and when he died a martyr's death, he left behind him a strong Christian community in Southern India from the Coromandel to the Malabar coasts. Brahminical persecutions soon began ; and in course of time the St. Thomas Christians largely availed themselves of the shelter afforded by the mountain fastnesses of the western coast to make their homes in Malabar. Here they remained for centuries, grew and multiplied, so that they became one of the recognised dominant races of the Malabar. The Nestorian heresy, however, got introduced into their midst, probably from Syria or Armenia ; and in course of time the whole community became Nestorians. When the Portuguese first came to India towards the end of the 15th century, they found these Indian Christians in a flourishing condition, respected for their soldierly qualities, and holding a high place among their heathen neighbours. They had Christian kings or Rajahs of their own, their own clergy, and an organised system of government which compared favourably with that of the surrounding heathen states. Sir William Hunter says:—"In virtue of an ancient Charter ascribed to Cherumal Perumal Suzerain of Southern India in the ninth century A.D., the Malabar Christians enjoyed all the rights of nobility. They even claimed precedence of the Nairs, who formed the heathen aristocracy. The St. Thomas Christians and the Nairs were in fact the most important military castes of the south-west coast. They supplied the body-guard of the local kings ; and the Christian caste was the first to learn the use of gunpowder and firearms. They thus became the match-lockmen of the Indian troops of Southern India, usually placed in the van, or around the person of the prince."

The downfall and degredation of these early Christian principalities in the Malabar was brought about by the Portuguese. In their eagerness to convert them to ortho-dox Roman Catholicism, not only did the Portuguese bitterly persecute them, but induced the surrounding heathen Rajahs to join them in their persecution. The Inquisition with all its horrors was introduced to assist in the conversion of these unfortunate indigenous Christians, and for a time Nestorianism was stamped out, and Roman Catholicism flourished in Malabar. But when the Portu-guese power declined, Nestorianism once more reappeared, but in a modified form ; so that the Malabar Christians are now partly Catholic and partly Nestorian in belief.

That this Christian caste did for centuries hold a high place for their warlike instincts, is undoubted ; and that they were largely employed both by Hindu and Mahomedan princes as soldiers is also undoubted. The brutal persecutions of the Portuguese however, largely crushed out their spirit. But the military spirit is not yet knocked out of them completely, as all officials who have had any dealing with them, speak well of their soldierly qualities ; and the pity is that in a province where good fighting material is scarce, more use has not been made of them. They number about half a million, so that the community is large enough to supply a good number of recruits.

Assamese Hillmen.—Ethnologically, the hillmen of Assam are Indo-Mongoloid ; that is, they are of mixed aboriginal and Mongol blood. They differ from other Indo-Mongoloids like the Garhwali and Khas in this, that whereas they are the race resulting from the fusion of aboriginal Indian and the Mongol, the Khas and Garhwal are of Aryan and Mongol stock.

Assam is said to derive its name from the Asms or Ahms, a tribe closely related to the Shans, who entered the province from the north-east and overran the whole of the Assam Valley. They continued the dominant tribe in Assam for several centuries, frequently coming into conflict with the Mahomedans. Ultimately they fell into decrepitude.

The principal tribes of Assamese hillmen who are of any military value are the Cacharis, Jharwas, Garos,

Nagas, and Abors. Most of these tribes have at some
time or other furnished some recruits to the Gurkha battalions localised in Assam before their conversion to pure
Gurkha battalions. They continue to supply recruits to
some of the Burma military police battalions, as also to
the military police in Assam itself. The opinion held of
them as regards their capabilities as soldiers is that they
are able to render useful service provided a very high
standard is not required of them ; but that they are far
from being thoroughly reliable material. Of these tribes,
the Cacharis, who are partly hillmen and partly resident
in the plains are perhaps the best for military purposes.
Of the several Naga clans, the Angami Naga and the
Kukis are the best. The Angamis are brave, warlike,
treacherous, fairly good looking, and of good physique.
The Kukis are numerically small, but are held in high
repute among their neighbours for their courage. The
Garos occupying the Garo Hills, are ugly to a degree,
but are considered brave. They are of good and sturdy
build.

Karens.—The Karens are a Mongol race more closely
allied to the Chinese than to the Burmese. Their original
habitat, according to their traditions, was west of the
desert of Gobi in Central Asia, from which they emigrated about the fourth century A.D., to their present
holdings. They are now found in parts of Siam, as
well as in Burma. They are partly hillmen and partly
resident in the plains, the plainsman being on the whole
superior to the hill Karen. The former is of good physique

and is not wanting in manly and warlike qualities. Their religion—despite the Buddhism of the dominant Burmese —is a primitive nature and devil worship ; but their traditions contain evidence of a former state when they were less barbarous than they are now. They have three clans among them, *viz.*, the Bghai, the Pwo, and the Sgau. There is now a large and flourishing colony of Karen Christians, brought into being by the efforts mainly of American missionaries. During the Mutiny these Christian Karens sent a loyal offer of help to the British Government, but the offer was declined. It is believed that from the Karen—whether heathen or Christian—some very fair material could be drawn. Karen Christians have done excellently in the Burma Military Police.

Ahirs.—The Ahir is an ubiquitous individual, for the caste is found all over Hindustan from Behar in the east, right away to the Indus on the west. The Eastern Ahir is of no use as a soldier ; the Ahir's martial qualities depend not on his caste but on the locality from which he is drawn. He is a cowherd, and in most districts is mainly employed in pastoral pursuits. They are however, now taking largely to agriculture, and in the Punjab they are mainly agriculturists. They are a hardworking, patient and industrious race, so that they are very well off. The Punjab Ahir is a splendid husbandman and is beaten by none. By religion they are mainly Hindu. His soldierly qualities depend very much on the locality from which he is drawn. Owing to the fact that the Ahir was once

dominant in the Rewari tahsil of the Gurgaon District—the
only locality in which he was ever dominant—the Ahir of
Gurgaon, and especially of Rewari, has more of the soldier
in him than those in other localities. The Ahir should
therefore be recruited from these tracts mostly, but some
good recruits could also be had in Rohtak, Patiala and
Eastern Rajputna. There are three main clans among them,
the Jadubans, Nandbans and Gwalbans. All Ahirs, no
matter where they reside, were originally of the same
ethnic stock ; and it is probable that they were originally
a nomad tribe of pastorals, probably Scythian, who entered India, *via* Persia and Baluchistan, early in the Christian
era. But there is not sufficient evidence to substantiate
this theory, though some of the traditions of the tribe
seem to favour it.

Brahmins.—In the Bengal Army there are two regiments of Brahmins, recruited exclusively in the N.-W. P.
and Oudh. Brahmins are of course, to be had all over
India, but, however diverse and scattered they may now
be, they all belong to the same stock. There are two
great divisions among them, the Gaur and the Dravira
or Dravida. The former comprise all Brahmins north of
the Narbudda, and the latter all south of it. There is
also this ethnic difference between them that the former
are almost pure Aryans, while the latter have a strain of
Turanian blood. Each class is divided into five tribes,
those of the Gaur being the Kanaujia, the Mithila, the
Saraswat, the Gaur, and the Utkala. The last are Brahmins of Orissa from whom no recruits are drawn. Each

tribe is subdivided into a large number of smaller divisions.

In the old Bengal Army, Brahmins were largely recruited, and did good service. The Kanaujia Brahmins of the N.-W. P. and Oudh supply excellent recruits ; and it is from this tribe that most of the recruits for the two Brahmin regiments are drawn. There are some 230 sub-tribes of the Kanaujia Brahmin.

The caste prejudices of the Brahmin reduce their value as soldiers. The great majority of the Dravira Brahmin tribes have no soldierly instincts whatever, and they are hardly enlisted.

The following titles distinguish the N.-W. P. and Oudh Brahmin from all other castes :—Dubé, Misr, Tribedí, Pandé, Chaubé, Agnihotri, Pathak, Awashti, Bajpai, Diksit, Sukul, Tiwari and Upadiya.

CHAPTER XIV.

MAHRATTAS.

A REFERENCE to the Indian Army List will show that the Bombay Army is very largely recruited from sources outside the civil limits of the Bombay Presidency. The Punjab, the frontier tribes, Rajputana, Central India, and even the North-Western Provinces and Oudh, are requisitioned for its material, and the recruiting area allotted to it is larger than in the case of any of the other three command armies.

The following are the races, castes, and tribes now enlisted in Bombay regiments and battalions :—

(1) Maharattas (Decanni and Konkani).

(2) Jats (of West and East Rajputana and Central India).

(3) Sikhs.

(4) Pathans.

(5) Rajputs (of Western Rajputana).

(6) Rajput Mahomedans (Rangars).

(7) Kaimkhanis.

(8) Punjabi Mahomedans.

(9) Mahomedans of Derajat.

(10) Baluchis.

(11) Mahomedans of Rajputana and Central India.

(12) Gujars.

(13) Mahomedans of the Bombay Presidency.

(14) Mers (of Western Rajputana).

(15) Hindustani Mahomedans.

(16) Hazaras.

Of these, the Sikhs, Pathans, Rajputs, Rangars, Punjabi Mahomedans, Mahomedans of the Derajat, Baluchis, and Hindustani Mahomedans enlisted in the Bombay Army are more or less the same as those already described as being enlisted into Punjab and Bengal regiments, and it is unnecessary to further describe them here. It should, however, be stated that Bombay also takes some classes of Sikhs (such as Ramgharia and Lohar Sikhs) which are not taken into any regiment in the Punjab ; and the same is the case with regard to Punjabi and Hindustani Mahomedans.

Mahrattas.—In early days Maharashtra was the name given to the tract of country bounded on the north by the Satpoora Mountains, on the east by the Waingunga and the River Wardha, on the south by the Godavery, and on the west by the Ocean. The name is probably derived from the Mahars, who are believed to have been the original inhabitants of the tract in question, but this is doubtful. The area of Maharashtra is somewhat over 100,000 square miles, and it is generally hilly, but in parts mountainous. The Western Ghâts divide it into two well-marked geographical divisions. That between the Ocean and the Ghâts is called the Konkan or Concan, and its width varies from 25 to 50 miles. The country east of the Ghâts is called in the vernacular, *Desh ;* but from the fact that it forms a part of the Deccan, it is not unfrequently known as the Decanni Mahratta country. Hence, for recruiting pur- poses, Mahrattas have been roughly divided into Konkani Mahrattas and Decanni Mahrattas ; and this division, though ethnologically incorrect, is geographically correct and suffices for all practical recruiting purposes. Since the rise of the Mahrattas as one of the ruling races in India, they have spread beyond the limits of the country known as Maharashtra, originally occupied by them ; and they are to be found well into the Central Provinces on the east, Central India on the north, and on the confines of Rajpūtana on the north and west. But the original home of the race is by far its best recruiting ground.

Of the early history of Maharashtra nothing is known for certain, but this is almost certain that the original inhabitants were not Aryans. It is also tolerably certain that, despite the fact that Mahratti is an Aryan language, the Mahrattas themselves are not in the main Aryan, but Turanian or Dravidian, with a strain of Aryan blood in them. The higher families doubtless possess a larger strain of Aryan blood than the rank and file, but the chances are that, as a whole, the Mahrattas are not Aryans. But it is always unwise to dogmatise on the subject of Indian ethnology, as the subject is so beset with difficulties ; and the only statement that can safely be made in regard to Mahratta ethnology is that they are probably a race who entered India from the north-west anterior to the Aryans, but were, on the entry of the latter, infused with a strain of their blood, as well as converted to their religion and to some extent their speech.

The inhabitants of Mahrashtra are, of course, all entitled to be called Mahrattas by virtue of their habitat in that locality. But this is giving the term Mahratta a

somewhat wider application than is given to it by the
people of Maharashtra themselves, because there are
several distinct ethnic elements in the population. The
Brahmins of Maharashtra, for example, will not class
themselves with Mahrattas, or rather, make a very
marked difference between themselves and other Mahrattas. The reason appears to be this. Hinduism was not
the original religion of the Mahars, who adopted it from
the Aryans. Aryan Brahmins came among these Mahars
and converted them to Hinduism ; and the modern Mahratta Brahmin is the more or less pure descendant of these
Aryan Brahmins who came to dwell among and convert
the Mahars. Hence, though classed with Mahrattas, these
Mahratta Brahmins are really ethnologically distinct,
and they preserve the knowledge of their origin by carefully distinguishing themselves from other Mahrattas
who are not ethnologically of Aryan stock. Again, Aryan
immigration into Maharashtra was not restricted to
Brahmins, but Rajputs or Aryan soldiers came as well ;
and the term Mahratta is sometimes restricted to the
descendants of these Rajputs, but they have a considerable strain of Mahar—*i.e.*, non-Aryan—blood in them. The
Koonbies, who are the Mahar peasantry of Maharashtra,
are also styled Mahrattas, and it is important to remember that it was these Koonbies who furnished most of the
Mahratta troops in their career of conquest.

Grant Duff in his History of the Mahrattas says it is a
mistake to suppose they were ever by instinct a military
race like the Sikhs and Gurkhas. But that does not

prevent them being made into good soldiers. The very fact of their having played so conspicuous and not always ignoble a part in the history of India, marks them out as a race with some of the qualities of the genuine soldier. The Duke of Wellington, who had such ample opportunity of forming a judgment in regard to them, rated them highly ; and there can be no doubt that with the discipline which the British officer enforces, and his personal example of courage, constancy, and devotion to duty, the Mahrattas can still be made into good soldiers, despite the enervating and softening influences which a long spell of peace appears to have on the Indian. The Mahrattas in days gone by had courage ; but it was the courage of the freebooter rather than the genuine soldierly instinct. They were at the best bold freebooters who were capable at times of courage because it paid them to be so ; but the moment the prospect of gain was taken away, their courage oozed out. The highest instincts of the soldier were never theirs. The loyal and stedfast adhesion to a good cause, which has led the highest human types in all ages to willingly sacrifice their lives, never inspired them. They were equally devoid of that spirit which takes death with proud indifference from motives of patriotism. The Mahratta all through his history has never risked a whole skin unless there was something very tangible and substantial to be got thereby, and many will doubtless commend his practical worldly wisdom.

He lacks the elegant proportions of the Jat Sikh, the sturdy, well-knit little figure of the Gurkha, the grand-

ly muscular build of the Pathan. He is cast altogether
in a less heroic mould ; but is constitutionally
sturdy, and can stand a good amount of exposure and
fatigue. The marching and re-cuperative powers they
displayed when General Wellesley was after them were
often prodigious. A correct estimate of the Mahratta as
a soldier would be that he is capable of rendering solid
and useful if not brilliant military service ; and that, with
careful recruiting and a personal interest in their welfare
on the part of British officers, the Mahratta would still
be, as indeed he was in days gone by, a credit to the
Indian Army. But it is always well to remember that
the Native Army will be just what its British officers make
of it, and that the excellence or otherwise of the material
of which it is composed is not the only determining factor.
For the influence of the stronger and manlier and higher
race must necessarily be an all-important factor in making
the Native Army fit for the strenuous duties which await
it sooner or later.

Mahratta history from the 16th century is treated
of in every school history of India, and it is unnecessary
to deal with it here.

APPENDIX.

Sub-divisions of the principal Pathan Tribes.

AFRIDIS.

(1) ADAM KHEL ...
- Ashu Khel ...
  - Ali Khel.
  - Kalla Khel.
  - Kandao.
  - Mahmadi.
  - Paradai.
- Hussun Khel ...
  - Jana Khori.
  - Akhorwal or Tatar Khel.
- Jowaki ...
  - Kimat Khel.
  - Haiybat Khel.
  - Bazid Khel.
- Galai ...
  - Yagi Khel.
  - Zargunt Khel.
  - Busti Khel.
  - Sharaki.

(2) KUKI KHEL ...
- Mita Khan Khel. {
  - Hussun Khel.
  - Asad Khel.
- Sikander Khel ... {
  - Usman Khel.
  - Zakku Khel.
- Abdal Khel ... {
  - Fateh Khel.
  - Madar Khel.
  - Khadak Khel.
  - Umar Khel.

(3) ZAKHA KHEL ...
- Badai ... {
  - Pakhai.
  - Zia-ud-din.
  - Anai.
- Nasr-ud-din ... {
  - Habib.
  - Paindai.
  - Khasrogi.
- Shanai

	Bah Bakhrai ...	Suran Khel. Jawakkai. Ghaibi Khel.
(4) SIPAH ...	Lundi Khel ..	Wund Gharai. Ibrahim Khel. Ali Khel. Abdul Rahim Khel.
	Urmuz Khel ...	Abdul Khel. Kaimal Khel.

	Malik-din Khel...	Umr Khan Khel or Mir Khan Khel. Kalla Khel. Ghalib Khan Khel.
(5) MALIK DIN KHEL ..	Khabi Khel ...	Hussun Khel. Hussein Khel.
	Karna Khel ...	Yar Muhammad. Durji Khel. Mira Khel. Altai Khel.

(6) AKA KHEL ...	Miri Khel Basi Khel. Sultan Khel. Mada Khel. Maruf Khel. Sher Khel. Sunial Khel. Mirghut Khel.

(7) KAMAR KHEL ...	Rarmi Khel. Yar Ali Khel. Shaikh Ali Khel.

(8) KAMBAR KHEL ...	Masti Khel. Pabbi Khel. Ambar Khel. Sheikhmal Khel. Shar Khel. Wali Beg Khel. Durbi Khel. Bash Khel. Khujal Khel. Mirza Beg Khel. Sarbadar Khel.

MOHMUNDS.

(1) BAR OR TRANSFRON-TIER ...	Tarakzai ...	Dadu Khel. Barhan Khel. Isa Khel. Kasim Khel.
	Halimzai ...	Busha Khel. Hamza Khel.
	Khwaizai ...	Dand Khel. Khadi Khel. Mehman Khel.
	Baizai ...	Babuzai. Usman Khel.
	Dawezai.	
	Kukkozai.	
	Utmanzai.	
(2) KUZ OR CIS-FRON-TIER ...	Kayakzai. Dawezai. Musazai. Sirganni. Matanni.	

ORAKZAIS.

(1) LASKKARZAI ...	Mamuzai. Ali Sherzai.
(2) DAULATZAI ...	Mahamad Khel. Bazoti. Utman Khel. Firoze Khel.
(3) ISMAILZAI ...	Akhel. Ibrahim Khel. Rabiya Khel. Mamazai. Isa Khel. Sadda Khel. Khadizai.
(4) STURI KHEL OR ALI-ZAI ...	Lalba Khel· Tazi Khel. Und Khel. Mala Khel. Anjari.
(5) MASUZAI ...	Khwaja Khel. Landazai.

YUSUFZAIS.

YUSUFZAI PROPER ...	Isazai ..		Hasanzai. Madazai or Mada Khel. Akazai.
	Iliazai ...		Salarzai. Nasozai. Ashaizai. Gadezai.
	Akhozai or Gauha		Baizai. Khwazozai.
	Malizai ...		Daulatzai. Nurizai. Chuggerzai.
	Ranizai ...		Ali Khel. Utmanzai. Sultan Khan Khel. Bahram Khel. Usman Khel.
MANDAUR ...	Razzar ...		Akozai. Mamozai. Malikzai. Manizai. Khidderzai.
	Utmanzai ...		Sadozai. Alazai. Kanazai. Akazai.
	Usmanzai ...		Kamalzai. Amazai.

WAZIRIS.

DARWASH KHEL ...	Ahmadzai ...		Shin Khel. Kalu Khel.
	Utmanzai ...		Mahmud or Mahmit Khel. Ibrahim Khel. Wali Khel.
MAHSUD ...			Alizai. Shaman Khel. Bahlolzai.

GURBAZ
LALI OR LELAI

ZAIMUKHT.

MAMOZAI OR MUHAM- MADZAI ...	{	Daudzai. Mandani. Manatuwal. Wattizai.
KOIDAD KHEL OR BAYUK ...	{	Hassan Khel. Tapai. Khadu Khel. Babakar Khel.

BANGASH.

BAIZAI ...	{	Karimdadi. Allahdadi. Bazadi. Malik. Miri.
JAMSHEDIS ...	{	Darsammand. Biland Khel. Bagzai.
SAMILZAI ...	{	Ilm Khel. Kagazai. Miwali. Landi Khel. Hassan Khel.
MIRANZAI ...	{	Umarzai. Hassanzai. Badda Khel. Surizai. Mandra Khel. Kha Khel.

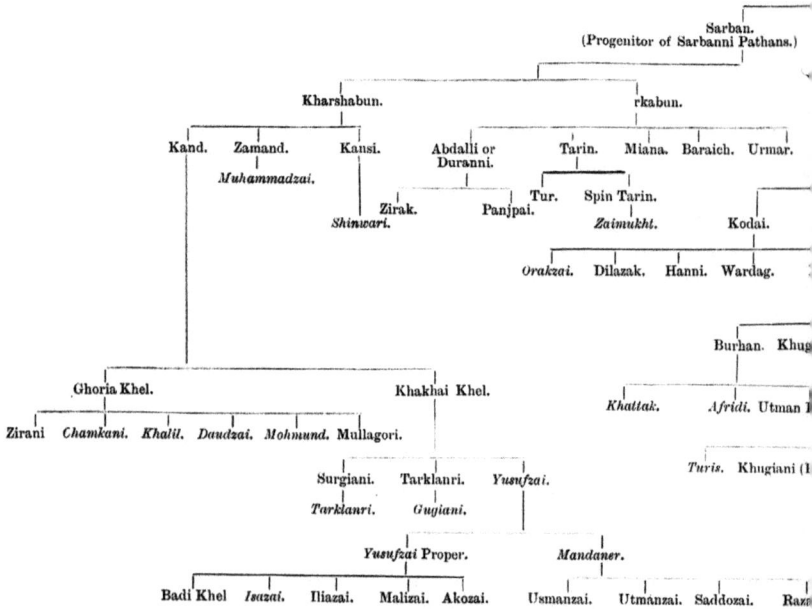

)N OF THE PATHAN AND AFGHAN TRIBES.

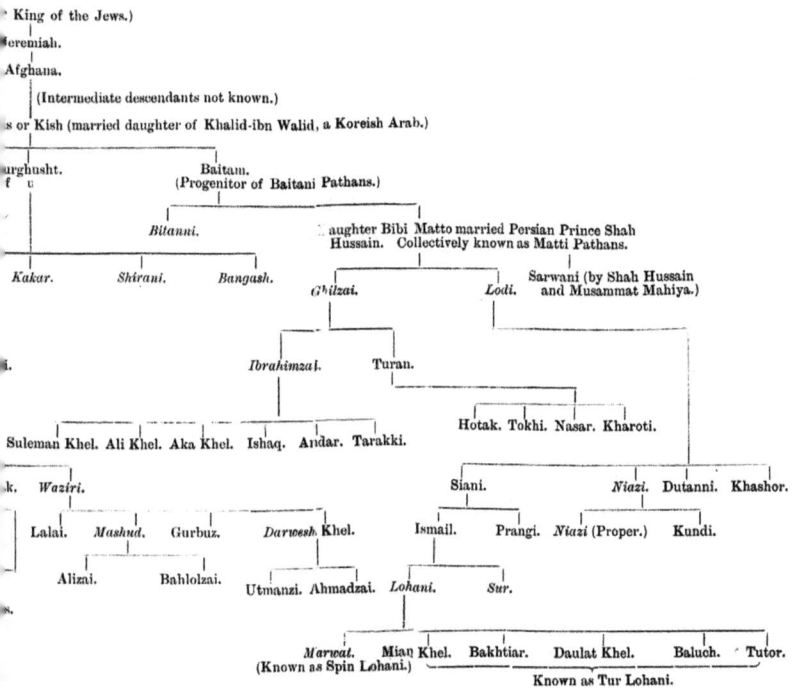

King of the Jews.)

eremiah.

Afghana.

(Intermediate descendants not known.)

s or Kish (married daughter of Khalid-ibn Walid, a Koreish Arab.)

urghusht.
f   u

Baitam.
(Progenitor of Baitani Pathans.)

Bitanni.

... aughter Bibi Matto married Persian Prince Shah
Hussain. Collectively known as Matti Pathans.

Kakar.   *Shirani.*   *Bangash.*

Ghilzai.   *Lodi.*   Sarwani (by Shah Hussain
and Musammat Mahiya.)

i.

Ibrahimzai.   Turan.

Hotak. Tokhi. Nasar. Kharoti.

Suleman Khel. Ali Khel. Aka Khel. Ishaq. Andar. Tarakki.

Siani.   *Niazi.* Dutanni. Khashor.

k.   *Waziri.*

Lalai. *Mashud.* Gurbuz.   *Darwesh* Khel.   Ismail.   Prangi. *Niazi* (Proper.)   Kundi.

Alizai.   Bahlolzai.

Utmanzi. Ahmadzai. *Lohani.*   *Sur.*

s.

Marwat.   Mian Khel. Bakhtiar. Daulat Khel. Baluch. ' Tutor.
(Known as Spin Lohani.)
Known as Tur Lohani.

INDIAN FRONTIER WARFARE
Major G J Younghusband
Drawing on the lessons of the Second Afghan War and the Chitral campaigns, this 1898 tactical treatise covers in much detail the methods of carrying on warfare on the difficult Indian Frontier. A scholarly work by a soldier who fought in the campaigns that he deals with in this excellent book.
9781783314812

A FRONTIER CAMPAIGN
The Viscount Fincastle, V.C.
and P. C. Elliott-Lockhart
Authentic account of the Field Forces operating on the NW Frontier of India 1897-98. Fincastle was awarded the VC during the Tirah campaign 1897 while serving with 16th Lancers.
9781845742560

THE HISTORY OF THE INDIAN MOUNTAIN ARTILLERY
Brig. Gen. C A L Graham
A first class history, covering the entire period from inception in 1840 through to post World War II operations in Indochina. Many officers, and some other ranks are mentioned in the text.

From 1850 onwards these highly mobile batteries based on mule transport and "screw-guns" that broke down into portable components that could be off-loaded & into action in seconds, were utilised in every North West Frontier campaign and overseas in The Great War (Gallipoli, German East Africa, Persia & Mesopotamia.) and World War II (Ethiopia, Malaya & Burma).
9781783311439

CAMPAIGNS ON THE NORTH-WEST FRONTIER
1851-1908
Captain Hugh L. Nevill, DSO, Royal Artillery
The single best one volume account of British campaigns against the tribes along India's North-West Frontier. It

covers in detail 27 frontier campaigns from the Black Mountain Expedition of 1852, to the Mohmand Field Force in 1908. Included are such campaigns as the 1863 Ambela campaign, the 1866 Black Mountain expedition, Jowaki 1877-78, Zakha Kel 1878-79, Mahsud 1881, Black Mountain 1888, 1891 Miranzi Field Force, the Mahsud Campaign of 1884-85, the 1895 Chitral Relief Force, the 1897 Frontier Uprisings with the operations of The Tochi, Malakand, Buner, Tirah, Peshawar and Kurram Field Forces.In addition to a detailed operational narrative, there are numerous appendices, including a list of British and indian regiments, with what campaigns each unit served in. This work is very helpful to British medal collectors for its information on these many small campaigns.

9781845741877

FRONTIER AND OVERSEAS EXPEDITIONS FROM INDIA:
A Series of 7 Volumes and 2 Supplements
Intelligence Branch Army Headquarters India

A splendid work of reference, highly readable, covering every border campaign and overseas expedition of the 19th and early 20th century.The first five volumes deal with the N.W.F., Afghanistan and Burma.Volume VI recounts the "Foreign" Expeditions to Africa, Ceylon, The Island of the Indian Ocean, Arabia, Persia, The Maldy Peninsula and China. Volume VII is devoted entirely to the Abor Campaign of 1911-1912.

Accompanying each combat account is a list of all the units engaged. This set of volumes forms an exceptional source of reference essential for any study of the British Military Presence in India.

N&M Press reprint (original pub 1911). HB. Complete in 9 Volumes, 3100pp in total , with 59 maps & illustrations. All volumes are available for purchase individually.
9781845743611